I0099167

ASK YOURSELF
Getting Back to Being Your Brother's Keeper
2nd Edition

By
Felicia Benton

PIAOTT Publishing LLC. Chicago, IL
Ask Yourself: Getting Back To Being Your Brother's Keeper
2nd Edition

ISBN: 978-0-692-75518-1

Second Edition: August 2016
First Edition: March 2015

First Published in Great Britain 2015 by Mirador Publishing

Copyright © 2015 by Felicia Benton

All rights reserved. No part of this publication may be reproduced
or transmitted, in any form or by any means, without permission of
the publishers or author. Excepting brief quotes used in reviews.

Any reference to real names and places are purely fictional and
are constructs of the author. Any offence the references produce is
unintentional and in no way reflects the reality of any locations or
people involved.

First edition copy of this work is available through the British
Library.

PIAOTT
PUBLISHING
A Limited Liability Company

Dedicated To My Mother

Thank you for teaching me not to take my problems out on people who definitely do not deserve it.

Thank you for teaching me to stop and think.

I Love you.

TABLE OF CONTENTS

Introduction

Even though a person may hear what you say, their reaction is the feeling they get from how you act.

STOP!

Take the time to read the introduction before you turn away. If by the time you are done, and you are not riddled with questions for yourself, then this is not the book for you. It simply means that, YOU ARE (or believe you are) your brother's keeper. Therefore, I am not talking to you and would like to thank you for any time taken. But, if, by the time you get done with the next few pages, and you pose important questions to yourself, then keep reading.

Humans naturally question their actions. It is hard-wired within our psyche to do so. But how many of us question the consequences of those actions?

"What will be the result if I do this?" Or "What will happen if I don't do that?"

This writer often wonders how many people truly question the consequences of their actions instead of the act itself, and what changes would happen to the world if everyone did.

What is the difference between questioning our actions and questioning the consequences?

The difference is, when we question our actions, we base the decision on our own feelings (on whether it is good or bad for us), but when we question the consequences of our actions we base the usage on how it affect others.

Ask yourself: Why is the world, at this current time, the way that it is? What is my part in the functioning of the present? Ask yourself: My actions - are they making the situation better or worse? Are my actions securing or destroying my future?

Being the curious person I am, I often wonder how my actions affect others. I don't know about you, but my actions clearly come back to me. It took a while to learn, but I found that what comes back is based on whether my actions were beneficial or harmful to another.

Many people in the world lost the concept of being a brother's keeper. What does being the keeper of your brother mean exactly? We see that phrase all of the time. It is mentioned at least 100 times in the Bible. Does it mean that we take a huge portion of our life and totally dedicate it to the happiness and well being of others? This writer does not think that's the case.

To be your brother's keeper is to work on being the best you so those outside of you do not have to suffer the consequences of your actions. In other words, if you are admittedly a person always late for an appointment or an occasion, no matter how hard you try to be on time, then you must realize that it is others affected by your actions.

How are they affected? I am glad you asked.

When your actions involve others, their reactions adjust as your actions are being manifested. Now you can say this statement is not true, but think about it. When actions and reactions begin to feed off each other, a chain of actions begins to form like a snowball. The chain start off small but gets bigger as it builds upon itself. This is commonly known as a chain reaction (a chain of responses that occur based on your initial action). Some of us may better know this as the butterfly effect. In theory, chaos theory to be exact, the butterfly effect is when a small change in one place can result in a change elsewhere but at a much more massive form (you have to look up the theory yourself. Maybe start with Wikipedia).

How many times when we are running late do we say to ourselves, "if I'm late this is really going to affect ......"

Why was this book written, and who am I?

I will tell you, "I am no one and everyone at the same time...someone who has not only questioned myself, but is asking you to do the same. I am no one to judge how we live our lives but I do have the right to ask why do we have to live with all of the problems of the world today: hunger, disease, murder, abuse, depression, anxiety, war, disbelief, mistrust, hatred, deceit, lack of care, sadness, homelessness, mean dispositions, evil intentions. I know full well that it is hard enough to live day to day without destroying our personal life and now this book is asking to consider those outside of our little box".

What nerve, who does this writer think he/she is?

At this point, you may be saying to yourself, "I'm not causing anyone else a problem; maybe they are the problem?" "Well, what is reading this book going to do, I'm just one person?" ...I am just guessing, but these may be some of the questions traveling across your mind as you read the introduction.

"I am a person who wants the lives of others to be better so that my life can continuously improve". This statement may seem selfish, but I thought about the consequences. What are the consequences? You may not want to continue to read. That statement could be interpreted as someone trying to sell another self-help book. I am actually trying to improve my life by helping you with yours. If by the time you get done reading this book and you began to think of how your actions affect others, and you start to live life in such a manner, then eventually, your chain of actions will reach me.

Want to read more???

Chapter 1

Talking To Self

Your conscience is your survival skill gauging the levels of care you hold for yourself and others. Your conscience is the keeper of the knowledge needed for consistent growth and development of your life.

According to the [1]PsychCentral website talking to yourself is a good thing. IT IS A SIGN OF SANITY. When you are talking to yourself you are looking within and allowing yourself to actually think.

Do you talk to yourself?

When you face a decision or you are about to perform some act, do you converse with yourself? Do you take the time to hold a serious conversation with that little voice inside before you make an important decision? You know the one called your conscience. That voice within is actually trying to stop you from doing something destructive to yourself or other individuals, so why not take some time to listen to it.

Let us not confuse the word conscience with conscious. I had to look up the differences. For clarity purposes, I included the meanings of both words.

> Conscious: aware, awake, alert, responsive, sentiment, compos mentis.
> Conscience: sense of right and wrong, moral sense, inner voice; morals, standards, values, principles, ethics, beliefs; scruples, qualms.

So it is OK to talk to yourself...your conscience. Sometimes we do not talk to ourselves because our conscience will automatically tell us if what we are doing is right or wrong. That is what it is supposed to do. Most of the time, however, it disagrees with what we want to do. Then we avoid what it is telling us. How many times have you said to yourself, I wish I followed my first mind? You feel bad because you know it was your conscience telling you which way to decide and you ignored what it had to say.

Your conscience is designed to always do the best for you. Ever think of it that way? Who will protect you better than you? Your conscience doesn't just protect you physically, but emotionally, mentally and morally. Your conscience is your survival skills, the levels of care you hold for yourself and others. Your conscience is the keeper of the knowledge needed for consistent growth and development of your life.

Why not talk to it? Get to know it. No one knows you better than you. Talking to your conscience is like a never-ending classroom with the subject being you. You will find out things you like, or truly love, what's not so cool, and things that you down right hate. But, at least you will know. All the facts will be on the table. One thing for sure, the more you get to know yourself, learn to accept your faults (we all have them) and laugh at yourself more, the easier your life becomes. When you talk to, follow and agree with your conscience, you learn to live a life free of regret.

> Regret: a feeling of sadness, repentance, or disappointment over something that has happened or been done.

Wikipedia calls it [2]intrapersonal communication. Now it is a well known fact that there are several mental diseases, defects and handicaps associated with talking to oneself. This is not the case here. That is a totally different book, written by someone else much more qualified to do so. I am simply touching on the health benefits of talking to yourself on a normal basis. Throughout this book, you will be asked to ask yourself questions, so you need to be comfortable with talking to yourself. It can increase the performance of your brain, enhance your attention span and regulate your decision-making skills. It helps to control how you respond emotionally and allows you to concentrate even with distractions.

If you haven't talked to your conscience before, try it. This is a conversation between you and you. Sometimes a second outer voice is needed while talking to yourself. Most of the time we only do it in our head (to ourselves). Give it an actual voice if necessary. I understand that most of us will be self conscious, because no one wants to be thought of as crazy, so go somewhere private. When or if someone see you doing this, and asks who are you talking to, just say, "We have to work something out." And when the look of confusion manifest on their face, you smile and say, "me and my conscience" (something clever of that nature). There is one thing you need to remember. When you are engaging in a conversation with self, don't be so hard and judgmental on yourself. Practice listening to yourself. Take the time to see what you find out. It is those times when you find out some very interesting facts. It helps you to organize thoughts, solidify goals and assist you in being the best you.

The Self-Esteem Exercise

Directions:
- Tear (cut) a sheet of paper into eight (8) pieces.
- Write a positive word and the numbers from 1 to 10 on each sheet and fold in half.
- Get two (2) small disposable bowls.
- Choose a day of the week. Write it on one of the bowls in large letters.
- Write the word finished on the second bowl.
- Tape the bowls together.

- Place all the pieces into the bowl with the week day written on it and mix them up.

- Set the bowls somewhere close to you (maybe your dresser or night stand).

The exercise:

- On the morning of the day you wrote on the bowl, close your eyes and pick a piece of paper.

- Open it and read the word. Then set to the side. Do not loose it you will need it later.

- Turn to a mirror and talk about the word to yourself. What it means and how to utilize it. Reflect on the word.

- During the week (until it is time for you to pick another word) use that word as much as you can. Either for yourself or for someone else. Try your hardest to act upon it.

- The night before it is time for you to pick another word, look at your word for that week and circle how you did (truthfully) on a scale of 1 to 10.

- Put that word in the finished bowl.

- Repeat until all the words are in the finished bowl.

- When done with all the words, add all the circled numbers together to see how close you come to eighty (80) points.

Here are the rules:

- Be completely honest with yourself.

- You can only look at the word twice. At the beginning and at the end of the week.

Your Score			
0–20	21–40	41–60	61–80
Negative Nancy	Keep Trying	The Right Track	Beam of Light

Chapter 2

WAKING UP!

When you wake up in a bad mood, try to work it out before you leave out the door. You can ensure that you will not transfer your negativity to the next person you come in contact with.

It would be utterly insane to ask people to wake up in a good mood every day and step out prepared to brighten another's day. So for the sake of reality, I will not even attempt to go that route. The truth is, we all have problems to deal with (some more than others) ….I will, however, ask you to contemplate how you appear to people when you walk out of your door. Do people ask you questions like, "What's wrong?" "Why are you frowning?" "I didn't do it!" "Why are you mad at me?" "I didn't sleep with you last night!" I know you either heard or said something similar.

What do these statements mean?

Well, if people are asking you anything close to those questions, then it could be how you allow your attitude to manifest when you wake up (I forgot to mention that our attitudes can affect our actions). When your eyes open what is the first thought? Is it what need to tackle through the course of the day (negative or positive) or is it, how blessed you are to even wake up? Now, even though this is a small change, forming that little amount of positivity can change the direction of our day. How, you ask? When your very first thought is appreciation for the fact that waking up can be easily taken away from you, everything else will seem insignificant.

We can all say, "I don't care how people see me, I have issues". Well now, there is that thing we do - thinking about ourselves… our actions and not the consequences - or better yet, the reactions. We walk out our doors with an uncaring attitude about people we "do not know" but let me give you something to chew on:

Scenario: YOU wake up in a bad mood. You get dressed to start your day. You go into a coffee shop still holding a bad mood. The clerk was in a good mood until they came across you. Now, the clerk is in a bad mood and is taking their frustration out on individuals behind you. In the clerk's line, however, the customer behind you was in a great mood, but now that has changed because of the terrible service they received from the clerk. Guess what? They are on their way to work. Because the clerk has been rude all day, the boss calls him/her into the office to talk, but the boss now picks up the clerk's bad attitude. The conversation escalates which leads to the suspension or even firing of the coffee house clerk. Even though the boss started off with a good attitude, it has changed. The coffee shop manager is now short-handed and has no choice but to work the other clerks even harder. The other clerks are upset and the entire atmosphere has gone in a downward spiral for the day. We must not forget about the customer behind you who received the rude service and is now going to work in a bad mood. Their day is now going downhill fast. They begin to notice little irritants (nuances like bad traffic began to form into big problems). Questions begin to flow through their head and out their mouths about the problems of the world. In actuality though, this person is still upset about the bad customer service they received earlier. Now let's say the customer who received the bad service earlier was someone in authority at his or her own job? The clerk has put this total stranger in a bad mood. Nearly everyone this person of authority comes across will have difficulties. Everyone has encountered a cranky manager, supervisor, court official, law officer, lawyer, etc. (...no offense) and had a difficult time.

Ok... Ok... Let us start again.

After going to sleep, we wake up with our first thought being about what happened before we went to sleep and how it is going to affect our current time. Some of us wake up and our brains immediately focus on what we have to conquer during the day. Hey...you know what? This writer does it too. I however will work real hard to do something on a daily basis. If I am in a bad mood when I wake up, I try to work it out before I leave out the door. I can ensure that I will not transfer my negativity to the next person I come in contact with. But, if I cannot work it out (gain some type of resolution), I make it a point to accept the mood I am in. I repeat to myself (almost to the point of chanting) that I will not "take it out" on people crossing my path.

You may begin to wonder, how does my simple act of waking up has anything to do with being my brother's keeper. Well, the way you wake up is simply the beginning boys and girls. If you make it a point to not to allow another individual to be affected by the trials of your life in any negative fashion then my friend, you are thinking about the next man. Focusing on starting your day in a good mood is an accomplishment. In today's society, thinking of the next man has become a privilege, instead of something embedded within our everyday actions. Up to this point, I've talked about us, strictly on a personal basis. But, what about the partner, parent, sibling, co-ed, or friend you share your life with. Have you ever wondered what is happening to him/her when you wake up in a bad mood? What happens to me when the shoe is on the other foot or as it is said, "wake up on the wrong side of the bed" You must ask yourself these questions if you are at all interested in the next man? Some would probably say in response, "I am not interested in the next man, only what's mine (family, friends, etc.)". The truth is however, your husband, brother, sister, mother, father, or friend is the next man...not to you, but to someone else.

Chapter 3

SMILE AND SAY HELLO

When you are not in such a good mood, switch your focus to making someone else's day brighter with a small act of kindness, like smiling.

It will make you feel better

This is a small chapter because it should not take a long time to talk about how a simple smile and a little hello or small nod of the head can go a long way. It is a sad thing to say, but we are a society afraid of its own shadow. There is so much hatred, bitterness and judgment towards one another that a simple gesture of kindness carries its weight in gold. You are probably saying to yourself, I smile and speak all the time. This chapter is not for you, so you can skip it if you choose.

But for those who do not find this chapter necessary, keep reading. Hopefully you will find something interesting.

The non-responder. Do you ask yourself, why is this person speaking to me? Or do you even look up? Do you say to yourself, "why are they being so nice, what do they want?"

Hey…non-responder. The person IS being kind.

The question I have for you and maybe you should ask yourself, why is it so hard for you to respond? Is there a problem with that person's race, gender, or age? Are too angry to spread a tiny amount of joy?

You probably do not realize how a non-response can affect another. Especially since you probably see them in passing. You may see the same individual on a daily basis, or you may never see that person again. But, how do you think that person felt when you did not respond to their gesture of kindness?

What if he/she spoke to 20 people and none of them

responded along with you. Do you think their moral would be brought down? Do you even care? Can you imagine being the one person that may brighten up their day with a simple smile?

Most times, you do not have to say a word...just give a signal of acknowledgment. Ask yourself, what is wrong with a little niceness? It may even make you feel better when you are not in such a good mood. It can break the ice. If you see someone who is clearly out of his or her element (i.e. new job) does it hurt if you smile at the person? The tiny motion is telling him/her everything is going to be ok. We all know how good it feels to see a friendly face in an unfamiliar environment. What if you notice someone around you is uncomfortable? You may be giving off a mean vibe from the look on your face. Softening your facial expressions and smiling can make someone warm up to you. It is only a suggestion.

Smiling can brighten your day. Lift your spirits up. If you woke up, got out of bed got dressed and left your home without feeling any better, try this. Switch your focus to making someone else's day better with small acts of kindness, like smiling. Eventually your problems may fall to the back of your mind and you begin to tell yourself your day is getting better. That turn of emotion comes from the responses of smiles you receive in return.

Chapter 4

OUR FAMILY

The truth is family is the concrete foundation for your life. If you do not take care of your family (your roots) to the best of your ability, then your base is not strong. That is the consequence for your actions, a weak foundation for your life.

Remember what I said in the introduction about chain-reactions, well every time you involve the next man, there is the start of a new chain. Whether or not it is a negative or positive chain depends on you. Imagine if we each of us actually worried about the consequences of our actions and how they affect others. What type of world would we really have? There are too many people who are not thinking about any other individual other than themselves and MAYBE their families.

Our family, our family… What is there to say other than… they are the only elements within our lives in which we are bound to love unconditionally. I know, I know… it is much more complicated than it sounds, but for some reason we are hard-wired to do so. So what are the consequences if we do not do our part (loving, improving, uplifting, building, etc.) in the family? Some would say none. "I am the only one who is going to live my life and deals with the consequences of my own actions. What I do has nothing to do with my family." Have you heard or said similar statements before? The truth is family is the concrete foundation for your life. If you do not take care of your family (your roots) to the best of your ability, then your base is not strong. That is the consequence for your actions, a weak foundation for your life.

Many of us are extremely confused about how some of our personal problems even exist. Let's go backwards for a minute. When you were between the ages of 3 and 4 (3 ½), your brain was like a sponge. Your curiosity was quickly climbing to the peak of your learning mountain. Everyone you came in contact with was prepared for your never-ending barrage of questions all starting with the word why. As you get older, the word why is not used as much. Time goes on and it becomes a word hardly used at all. You stopped your questioning. Going backwards is to dig deep and pull that inquisitive 3½-year-old child. Start using the word why again. Not like the conservative adult who likes to preserve their dignity, but out loud like a child.

Why do we may act and/or react the way that we do? Why do we get irate about a situation so insignificant to our existence? Why we allow the simplest solution to a problem getaway from us? Why do we procrastinate? Why is our opinion about love, society, work, religion, etc. the way it is? Why do we view at a particular race of people with confusion or hatred? Why do we feel the way we do about drugs, sex, alcohol, music and the arts?

These are questions we should be asking ourselves on a regular basis. By asking these pertinent questions, we can develop a focus on our own grounding and positive contributions to society without plaguing the world with our family hang-ups. We tend to blame the next man for our experiences (only the negative stuff). But, at some point, we must take the time to look really deep within ourselves and check the roots. Sometimes you should question the values being taught. Currently as a societal whole, we are on an increasing rate of families decreasing in strength, numbers, and unity. Today you can hardly tell who is related. There was a time when family was everything. Families did not rape, kill, harm, mistrust and sue each other as frequently and easily as we do today. The projection of family was so strong that the neighbors even chipped in to help. Today a neighbor cannot correct a child that is not theirs without running into confrontation with the parents. Even if the child is clearly in the wrong. Remember the old saying, "it takes a village to raise a child". Well, that concept is clearly gone. So what do we do? Do we go back to the old ways (as if it's even possible)? Do we try to come up with solutions (individually and as a whole) that can possibly take us back to being our brother's keeper? What can the solution be? Can we trust each other again? Well, in my opinion, it starts with the family.

Strengthening your family is a big part in being your brother's keeper. Each and every one of us has a family member (or members) who tries to take the family and stomp it into the ground. It is usually the disruptive, angry and uncaring family member who has the most impact on what goes on in the family.

What do I mean?

I mean the cousin that steals, or is violent every time he/she comes to the family functions. I mean the uncle, father or nephew who is a predator preying on the nieces and daughters. I mean the aunt or grandmother who does not approve of new members because they don't "fit" into their criteria. They're the ones who always cause commotion and rumors because they don't like the new wife or husband. I mean the daughter, sister, brother or son, who has decided that drugs, alcohol, lying, cheating or promiscuity is the way to go. I mean the mother or father taking their anger out on their children especially when they don't deserve it. I'm even talking about the snot-nosed little kid in the family who is bad as they come. You hate to see him/her coming because you know they are going to get into, tear up or break something. The parent is not going to do anything about it. Well to all of the individuals I mentioned, there are six words to say to you...

STOP IT! YOU ARE DESTROYING THE FAMILY!!

Do you care? I would say obviously not. If you are participating in any of the previously mentioned behaviors (or ones I did not mention, but are horrible), then you are definitely not thinking about anyone but yourself.

> Scenario: A mother loves her son. Over the years, he grows to be a good son who always helps her. As he develops into a man, he gets closer to his mother and has a deep respect for her opinion. One day this son meets the woman of his dreams. As this new relationship develops, he finds her to be sweet and loving. He finds many of the same qualities in her his mother has, and comes to love her deeply. He decides it was time for the two leading ladies in his life to meet. Instantly the mother does not like the woman that her son is now in love with. There is no viable reason as to why she dislike the woman, she just know this woman is spending too much time with her good son. She does not share this information with her son because believe the relationship will not last. Much to the mother's dismay, the son decides to marry the woman. Over time, she is not being honest with her son or respecting his decision to marry this woman. She shows her unhappiness of the marriage only to the wife, never to her son. The wife repeatedly expresses to her husband his mother's disapproval of their marriage. She explains to her husband about how her mother-in-law's consistently embarrasses her when they go to family functions (a practice she started at their wedding). Every time the wife mentions this to him, it invokes an argument. The husband refuse to believe his mother, the woman of whom he trust

and love would ever dislike his wife, especially since she never told him. As time goes on, the arguments get worse and worse. Eventually, they separate and both are miserable.

What do you think the outcome would be if the mother told her son she was not fond of the woman he married? What if the mother trusted her son's decision and tried to get along with his wife? Would the scenario ended differently?

I am no angel. My actions are not always so beneficial to my family. That is why this section is included. Sometimes we cannot control what we do...no matter whom it hurts. But again, this writer is only asking you to pay very close attention to your actions, and realize who is going to be there when you fall (and we all do). The one thing that all Family Abusers (my own term) have in common is the enormous egos possessed. What is an ego anyway?

> Ego: Self-esteem: somebody's idea of his or her own importance or worth, usually of an appropriate level; Inflated opinion of self: an exaggerated sense of self-importance and a feeling of superiority to other people; A part of mind containing consciousness: in Freudian psychology, one of three main divisions of the mind, containing consciousness and memory and involved with control, planning, and conforming to reality.
>
> Thank you for the definition Bing.com

Now ask yourself...should our egos play any part in our family interactions? When the ego is put to the side and time is taken to think about the affect my actions has on other family members, their reactions to my actions are not so devastating. I will change decisions based on if it will hurt someone in the family. Some of us cannot see ourselves doing changing a decision based on someone else's feelings. But isn't it funny how things workout? When true care is put into a decision and we cross all of our T's and dot all of our I's then the decision we make usually ends in being the right one for the family. It may not be a very easy task, but when your roots become stronger instead of weaker based on your actions, the reward makes all the work that is put in well worth the effort.

Chapter 5

WORK LIFE

Week in and week out, we all, regardless of position, work together. It is all within ourselves to be our brother's keepers and the workplace is one area in which we can practice this the most.

Work...Work...Work...Work.

This one is for the working stiff. This can be any one of us. From the individual who sits at the board meetings and make important decisions "best for the company" to the coffee house clerk giving us our cup of morning Java...Latte...Espresso, or whatever floats your boat.

Within our lifetime, there are certain things required for our absolute survival. Eating healthy, getting the accurate amount of sleep, drinking plenty of water, exercising...Aww and the most important one...The one that isn't discussed very often as our means of survival...WORK!!! Let's face it. If it were within our power we would all be rich and comfortable with no problems. Each of us would like it if we did not have bills to pay and we can acquire everything our hearts desired with the snap of our finger.... ... ...And now we wake up! In reality we must work...even if you consider yourself to be financially sound. You have to continue working in order to stay that way.

Now that's out of the way, it is time to start asking some questions. Ask yourself, how do I handle adversity at work? If something negative happens at the beginning of the week, do I carry it with me for the whole week? Do I take my issues out on the people I work with?

I don't know about you, but I was guilty.

It is the first day of the week. Based on what went on last

week or the previous weekend we often say to ourselves, next week is already pre-destined. The week will continue on the same path. Well, what I've learned in my experiences, my good people, is that the chain-reaction to my actions can be balanced and controlled.

Here's the reason I decided to put this section in the book.

The working individual can be the most inconsiderate person in the world (myself included). Why do I say that? Well, let us think. When we are at work, in truth, we are only focusing on our situation. The very last thing that we are trying to be is our brother's keeper. Throughout the day thoughts consistently swirl around our brains about how we will spend our check at the end of the pay period. We concentrate on our work performance so the boss is impressed. Hopefully getting him/her to notice so they can remember you when it is time for a raise. We keep our eyes on the clock wishing that time will fly so the day is over. We ponder over what we have to do when we get off work. We will even take into account individuals we work for - but not whom we're working with...

Our co-workers.

WELL, WHAT ABOUT OUR CO-WORKERS?

They are just people we work with day in and day out.

Most of us do not think past that point. But we should. As I said before, we only concern ourselves with what we need to do to ensure our own survival. When was the last time you stopped and thought about your co-worker? We do not even realize how much interaction there is with the individuals we work with, and how much affect we have on each other lives.

So what can be the consequences for not considering our co-worker?

The answer is an unhealthy, uncomfortable, tense and

unfair work environment. There are higher stress levels for everyone involved. One of the leading causes for deadly illnesses is stress. You know them... heart disease, stroke, weight gain, etc. So what do you do?

The first thing is asking some hard-core questions:

What part do I play in my work environment?

Is it positive or negative?

Do I bring my personal problems to work? Is it hard for me to enjoy my job because of my personal problems?

Am I doing my job to the best of my ability?

Am I honest about my abilities? Can I really do what I said I can do or am I only looking to get paid?

Am I an ass kisser? (You may not want to ask that question) Why do I kiss the bosses' ass?

Do I like my job? (The actual job) Am I good at my job?

Why did I make the last two questions bold? They are the most important questions you as an employed person can ask. Not enjoying your work or being good at your job can cause one of the largest negative chains of reactions in a work place. What do I mean??

Let's say, you get no joy from your job. It can be a surefire bet that at some point you will take this fact out on the people you work with and/or for. The ones who really catch your wrath are the ones happiest with the position they are in. Is it really fair for people who work around you have to deal with your attitude and displeasure for the job? Better yet, who wants to work in an environment where there is no trust in or from your co-workers? It can be quite disturbing when you are paranoid about your co-worker on a daily basis. Your work place becomes extremely uncomfortable when you feel they are out to sabotage you and your efforts. Even worse, they think you are the saboteur.

Do we even realize the amount of joy, teamwork, and progress being held back because of the tension?

The biggest problem is that most of us only think of ourselves. When we do that and don't think about the people we work with, we tend to (unknowingly) stoop to levels that we normally would not go.

Let's start with rumors. Yeah, it is a BIG ONE!

Have you ever said anything negative (no matter how small or harmless) about your co-worker to another co-worker? Be honest with yourself... no one knows what you are thinking and feeling as you read this book unless you tell someone.

The smallest negative comment could start a rumor. Negativity travels much faster than positivity. Unfortunately, in today's society we are quick to spread the bad stuff. When you make negative comments to someone about another person, you run the high risk of he/she telling another individual. It turns into a vicious cycle. The truth gets buried and someone always get hurt.

> Scenario: Joan and Debra works in department C of Paperclips Office Supply Store. One day, Joan decided to confide in Debra. Trusting her as a friend, Joan tells Debra about a secret crush she has on the supervisor, Jack. She goes on to tell Debra that she would really like to date him and they flirt with each other from time to time. But, because of the company's strict policy, they have refrained from expressing their feelings openly. Debra doesn't say much and remain impartial. She's being a friend and listening. The next day, however, Joan is off of work. Debra, on the other hand is there. All day she has wanted to burst at

the seams with the information Joan told her the day before. Not remembering her friend privacy, she decides to tell Andrew of Department E (way on the other side of the store). Now, since Debra was so focused on the gossip, it slipped her mind about Andy being jealous of Jack's success in the company. He saw this as a great opportunity to get Jack fired and take his job. Andy, fueled with important information, tells a few people in the store. He twisted the story to make it seems as if Joan and Jack had been having a torrid affair for months. This information soon finds its way to human resources. After a few days, Joan and Jack are called into the office and actions are being implemented due to fraternization. Because Debra did give any forethought about the consequences of her actions, two people lives are turned upside down and jobs were lost.

Ask yourself, what would you do differently? Have you ever been a confidant and betrayed that confidence? If so, did you understand the reactions to your action? Well, I realized the results are never pretty so I decided to change. What about you?

To the captains of industry... the corporate bosses, managers, and employers of others. There is one question that I (and probably everyone that has a boss) would like the answer to. Would you work for you?

This is a question that generally crosses your employee's mind. We also wonder if you ask it on a regular basis. If you can truly, within yourself answer with an honest yes, then don't worry about the next question.

Am I a good boss?

If you answer no (if your ego allows it), then maybe you should consider what type of person you would like to work for. Week in and week out, we all, regardless of position, work together. It is all within ourselves to be our brother's keepers and the workplace is one area in which we can practice this the most. On an average, we spend at least 8 hours at work, 5 days a week (not including overtime or special circumstances). 40 hours per week. Three months equals to 120 hours, which is equivalent to five 24-hour days you spend with the people you work with. In a year, that is 60 days. A little more than 16 percent of your life each year is spent with these people. When you have the chance, look at www.bls.gov/tus/charts/. It is the United States Department of Labor's Bureau of Labor and Statistics website. Check out where your time goes. Imagine the possibility of 16 percent of your life stress-free?

Chapter 6

TGIF

If you work Monday thru Friday, do you respect those that don't?

Hey! Alright! WooHoo! It's Friday! What is so different about Friday in comparison to the rest of the week? You ever asked yourself? Everyone is always excited on Friday "...it's the end of the week". Well, I say not for everyone. Some believe Saturday is the end of the week. What about them? I'm wondering why we choose Friday to be a little nicer, breathe a little easier, spend a little bit more money or ready to party. Why can't we be the same way on Tuesday or Thursday?

Wake up people. It is the end of the week for some who work or go to school from Monday thru Friday. What about the people whose workweek is from Thursday thru Monday? Their weekend starts on Tuesday. Now, let me ask you, Wednesday is the middle of the week for you. Is the person who is off (because it's their weekend) deserving of your attitude? You still got a few days to go before you're off.

Why do some of us decide Friday is the day we will get wild? Don't believe me, next time you're out and about, pay attention. People drive faster and more sporadically, talk louder, are a little easier with how much they spend, smile more, are nicer, flirtier, etc.

> Scenario: It is Thursday morning. Neighbors Jeffery and Michael wake up to start their day. Michael gets up with a spring in his step, smiling and happy. Jeffery has a completely different mood. He is somber and stern...a little grumpy

even. When they see each other, neither man take the time to speak. They are each wrapped in their thoughts. Nothing negative happened to either man the day before. As a matter of fact, Jeffery had the day off. Michael on the other hand had to work. So why the dramatic difference in their attitudes? Why is it Michael and not Jeffery in a good mood? Well, for Michael Thursday marks the day before the end of the week. For Jeffery however, it marks the day before the beginning of a long and grueling week of work.

It is Friday, the next day.

Jeffery is in a better mood due to going to bed early and getting a good night rest. He loves his job, but know it will be a long and tiring week. He's dragging along, taking his time and contemplating the tasks ahead. Michael on the other hand, has one thought in mind. He repeatedly says to himself, "I just need to make it through the day... it's FRIDAY...party time!" He's rushing around, trying to hurry and get to work on time. Ironically, Michael and Jeffery make it out the door at the same time. Michael sees Jeffery and screams "GOOD MORNIN NEIGHBOR" in a very excited voice. Jeffery waves, but frowns at Michael's loudness. He grumbles to himself, "he's only like this on Fridays. I hope he's not going to be loud this weekend. He always forgets that I work on Saturdays and Sundays." Michael likes to party on his days off. This is something happening every week with these neighbors. And today was the day Jeffery wanted it to end.

The end of this scenario can only go two ways... positive or negative. Let your imagination do the walking. The ending you conclude could be based on how you conduct yourself on your day off and how you are to your neighbors.

Do you know anyone personally who do not work a typical workweek of Monday thru Friday? If you work Monday thru Friday, do you respect those that don't? In other words, are you as easygoing on Wednesday as you are on Friday? Is your attitude completely different because it's in the middle of your workweek? Do you pay attention to those around you on your day off?

Just ask yourself those questions on your day off and apply them in the middle of your workweek. Use it as an experiment to see what happens. Try doing this for about a month. You might be surprised on how much your attitude may or may not flip. If the experiment is successful, the amount of things like road rage, accidents, fighting, arguing, negativity, etc. may lower in your life. Eventually, you develop a since of evenness on how you treat others as you pay more and more attention to how you conduct yourself on a daily basis.

Some would say that this chapter is silly due to the perceived insignificance of the subject matter. But, think about this for a second. If you are angry about regular life (work, bills, responsibility) six days out of the week and Friday is the one day of the week you are genial, affable, cordial, friendly, amiable, easygoing, approachable, good-natured, cheerful, cheery; companionable, comradely, sociable... Then I have news for you. There are typically 53 Fridays in a year. That is it. Which means that the other 312 days of the year, everyone around you have to deal with your attitude and anger. Would you consider that fair?

The Reflection Page

Here is where you check your personal mirror and write down what you see about yourself.

Subject: The Way I Treat Others.

In my mirror, I see:

_____

_____

_____

_____

_____

_____

_____

_____

_____

_____

_____

_____

_____

_____

_____

_____

_____

_____

_____

_____

_____

Chapter 7

THE COMMONS

By actually participating and paying attention to what is generally said to be common, you move along the path of being your brother's keeper. Focusing on the common things leaves little room for judgment of our differences.

Common: Occurring, found or done often, prevalent.

The word is a description of all cultural and natural resources accessible to everyone. You know them, supposed common things like water, a healthy place to live, or a happy existence. But, these days, we even try to privatize and charge money for the gifts nature gives us, like air (e.g. oxygen in hospitals, air pumps, airplane oxygen), hence making even these commons not so common.

Common... to be shared among all...

Well, what is common these days? Let us explore this. Strike out resources. You get the best resources, natural or otherwise, when you have the money to pay for it. Maybe it is our common sense.

I hate to tell you this, but common sense is quickly becoming something quite uncommon. According to the New Oxford American dictionary, it is the basic ability to perceive, understand and judge things which is shared by people and can be expected reasonably without debate. So... why is it called common sense again? Now if that phrase was true to the definition, then everyone should posses it, which means everyone should be using it. The problem with that philosophy is that we only act, or react to things that make sense to us. So where is the commonality?

55

There is no definition for common courtesy, but we can define it. We know the meaning of common, as it was stated earlier. According to the New Oxford American dictionary, courtesy is "excellence of manners or social conduct; polite behavior, a courteous, respectful, or considerate act or expression. Indulgence, consent, or acquiescence: favor, help, or generosity."

We can now say common courtesy is defined as everyone having excellent manners. Is it common practice to use common courtesy?

How much do you practice it?

It is understandable. With the way the world is today, it is difficult to use the action of common courtesy, but it makes you feel better to be kind. If you believe in karma (and you do not have to), you should know kindness comes back to you in return. I included that little example of how a simple common courtesy practice can be greatly overlooked.

The person behind you in the grocery line has one item and you have twenty. The other lines are either closed or very long. Well, what will happen if you let he/she ahead of you? Do you just turn your back because you were there first?

The common good: the benefit or interest of all.

What do we have, or, what is done for the common good? Is it religion or politics? Maybe it's the justice or healthcare systems? You tell me, because I can't figure it out. Now, I know these entities are supposed to be for the common good, but as we see every day, that is not the case. At this point, you may feel I am being a cynic, but I am truly not. I only need answers and you should want the same.

Ask yourself: Should the word "common" be stricken from the dictionary? Or should we start with something simple, like learning about our commonalities. By actually participating and paying attention to what is generally said to be common, you move along the path of being your brother's keeper. Focusing on the common things leaves little room for judgment of our differences. At the end of this paragraph, stop and use your imagination for a minute. Imagine if we used he commons. We would actually do things for the common good on a regular basis. So much so, it becomes common practice. How do you think this world would be? I would say like a well-oiled, smooth running machine.

I came up with this statement..."Let us get on common ground by choosing common courtesy and developing some common knowledge about our common practices. Then, we can enforce common laws for the common good with a common cause, a common goal, and a common theme, therefore, binding our common thread to solve the common problem."

PRACTICING COMMON COURTESY

Please And Thank You

This is something that seems to be very difficult for some people these days. But saying please and thank you goes a long way. Have you ever done something nice for someone. It could be something as simple as holding the door open for them. Do you remember the feeling of ungratefulness you received simply because they did not say those words. Well, think. Every time you do either refuse or forget so say those small words, that person that helped you has that same ungrateful feeling coming from you. Saying please and thank you speaks to you character

Smiling And Hello

This is another small gesture that is so simple, we overlook it. Even if you give a half smile due to you having a terrible day. That half smile tells the receiver... "Hey, I acknowledge you but I am having a bad day." Then the person passing you or trying to be kind will not feel some type of way.

Remember Your Surroundings

We get so wrapped up in our own world that we forget about everything around us. Think about people walking behind you. It is simply rude to walk through a door busy with traffic and you do not at least attempt to hold the door open. You know what the person behind you is thinking...YOU ARE RUDE! It does not take a lot of time or energy to do. To allow a door to slam in a person's face is one of the ultimate forms of disrespect.

Rushing To Beat A Person

Why do we rush to beat each other? Sometimes I can understand a parking space close to the door but even that do not constitute a cussing and arguing. Even worse, a fight. Our fuses have become so short that we will fist fight someone over a parking space. What I cannot understand is, why do we rush to beat each other through a door? Are things in the world today this serious that we will hurt each other over these simplicities? Think about it the next time you get upset when someone get to the door or that parking space before you.

Help Someone Out

If you see someone struggling with a lot of bags, ask if they need help. If you are in a rush, as many of us are...every day of our lives, then it is understandable if you do not have time. But sometimes when you know you have a few extra minutes, it doesn't hurt.

Drop Your Ego A Bit!

Ok! So you had a long and tired day. You are not exempt, all those around you in that environment may feel the same as you do. So please, if you are in a crowded area, move over. Move your bags from the empty seat. Shift your feet from the middle of the isle. Your body language can say a lot to the person in eye contact with you. Your gesture of non compliance to the environment is another way of not showing common courtesy.

Kindness Begins At Home

What we do at home. How we treat each other within our own dwellings is often spilled in the streets. This is the best place to practice common courtesy regularly. Drop the attitude about helping your parents, siblings, children or spouse. If you have a problem at home being kind, then there is no way you can be kind in public and be genuine about it.

Be Kind To Your Environment

You do not have to go out and plant trees all over the world unless that is your preference. You can care for your environment by finding a trash can and not throwing your trash on the ground, Even if you do not understand the recycling process. It shows a great lack of care for yourself and where you live each time you throw your trash on the ground. Just hold it until you come across a trash can. They are everywhere.

Chapter 8

WHAT'S IN A NAME

"The next time I see the name before I meet the person, I will not judge."

"The next time I see the name before I meet the person, I will not characterize."

"The next time I see the name before I meet the person, I will not discriminate."

Reading a newspaper, I came across the name Marijuana Pepsi. This is actually someone's name. At first I, like so many others, made quick judgments. I left it alone at first, but the name stuck in my head because it was so unusual. I wanted to know what type of person is able to carry such a name. I was so curious about what type of life they had, and how bold his/her parents were. With no intent of intrusion or malice involved, I lightly researched this person. I was pleasantly surprised. She is a very beautiful educator with a master's degree in higher education administration, which overcame the odds of having a unique name. She deserves nothing but the highest respect and admiration. I found myself saying keep up the good work. I will admit, however, in the back of my mind I said, "WOW, with that name, I would not have ever thought". I asked myself, if I could have been as strong? It was the birth of this chapter.

This may seem like a crazy chapter once you read it. But, ever wondered how much thought was actually given to the names of some people.

For men and women, having a baby is a huge life-changing event. From the moment that we find out that we are pregnant, our minds begin to reel with plans. The first thought is how we can make life better for the new addition to the family. But, while we are thinking of getting a bigger place to live, a better car, or a higher paying job, are we thinking of how the name can effect his/her future? Do you realize that a name can be the initial guide toward the success or downfall of a person? I put **can be** in bold so that you, the reader, understands that this is just info based on my own research. There is actual scientific research, so this subject is not something I pulled out of the air. One day while you are browsing the web, go to the [3]Live Science website.

When people introduce themselves, do you judge their personality or qualifications by their name? Or better yet, ask yourself, am I embarrassed when I tell people my name? Have you ever said to yourself, "What were my parents thinking when they named me?"

One day when you have time, read [4]The Impact of Your Name. It is an ABC 20/20 online article written by John Stossel and Katrina Kendall. A video titled Is Your Name Helping Or Hurting You? goes with the article.

I am going to put it all on the table. We all need to ask ourselves, why do we characterize, judge and/or discriminate based on a person's name? You may be saying to yourself, "I don't think like that". But, deep down you do...I do...I am not going to lie to you. It's not something I am very proud of. So not to make this a long and drawn out chapter, I will share my mantras:

> "The next time I see the name before I meet the person, I will not judge."
> "The next time I see the name before I meet the person, I will not characterize."
> "The next time I see the name before I meet the person, I will not discriminate."

Now it is my opinion (and it is just my opinion), but if we get these thoughts ingrained in our systems, the next time we see names like JaQuann or Shaniqua we won't think they come from the ghetto. When we see names like Becky or Jen we will not automatically think ditzy blonde. Maybe we will not think terrorist if we hear a name like Barack Hussein Obama or Abdul Hafeez. Let us make a silent vow to ourselves. We will we get to know the person before deciding (based on their name) what type of person they really are.

Do you, reader, believe there could ever be a time when a hiring manager won't stop at the name of an applicant?

Though most people in authority won't admit it. Judging a person based on their name is constantly practiced within the working world. As a matter of fact, a variety and sometimes very important decisions has been made with the deciding factor being a person's name.

We have to change that.

You ever turned away a candidate because you saw their name? Did you automatically feel they were not qualified? If the answer was yes, and remember this is between you and you, then you may have turned away possibly the best worker, renter, business partner, student, etc. You made this decision based on something completely out of their control. It is as simple as that.

So I say to you, the public (myself included), don't worry so much about the name. Start checking the qualifications first. Get to know the person. Then look at the name. You may be surprised.

Many scientist and reports states that our name determines many factors about us. In my opinion, your name determines one thing... Your nationality. Your race. And it is those two things that attributes to all other factors, hence classification.

In this day and age it is confusing as to why we are still classifying a person according to their name. We can agree that each race of people have a mixture of another culture within it. No race or culture are of the purest of nature. Why would you waste time on the name of the person unless you choosing to judge them. Judging people by their name is no different than stereotyping.

Challenge: Get To know People Names

Everyone has one or more person that we have made a judgement upon based on their name. We do this because of the stereotypes surrounding our every understanding of different cultures. If you are serious about getting to know people without judging them by their names, then here is a challenge for you. The next time you meet someone new and their name seem strange to you. Before you judge, ask them where their name came from. Make a mental note of their answer and write down your feelings about their name in the first section below. If possible get to know that person and revisit this page in a few weeks. Then write down your feelings about the person and see the difference.

Today I met a person named_____.
His/her name made me feel:

I have had the chance to get to know_____.
I have learned this about them:

Chapter 9

MUSIC...REALLY???

Try to remember what the music did for you. We need to realize that each generation has a language. Equipped with a way of understanding that language. This is the language they use in their music.

What happened to the music? It's not the same as it was back when I was that age. Sounds familiar? Ever said something similar?

Guess what…it's not going to sound the same. You should know that. Of course, the music of your generation will sound better to you. It is my guess that you were a teen in the 70's. You believed the music during that period had meaning. They had something to say.

Here is the point of this chapter…I am willing to bet that the children, teens, and young adults of this time believe the exact same thing about their music. And, your parents felt the same way about the music of their time.

We need to ask ourselves: Why are we so quick to judge the music being played today? This generation understands it even if you don't.

Now don't get me wrong. I've gotten in my car, checked my mirrors and prepared myself to leave for my destination. But, before pulling off, I like millions and millions of people turn on the radio. I was looking for music to aid me in my journey. After five minutes of flipping through the radio stations, I begin to think to myself, everything on here is bull****. I am so thankful for CDs and iPods. I instantly plugged my iPod into the connector and played only music I wanted to hear.

One day, it came to me; I was stuck in my era. How and when it happened, I cannot tell you. But it did happen. I found myself sounding like my mother when talking to my children about the music "these days". I had to ask myself, when did I become so closed-minded? When did I start to believe that, the music of my time was the best music ever and nothing else of any era can compare?

We don't recognize it, but at some point we all become frozen in time (unconsciously of course). We take the best portion of our life and associate everything from that time to be the best. Have you ever said, "this was so much better when I was little"? Or, when it comes to music, "man, when I was a teen, people had something to say. I don't know what's going on with the music today." Well my friend, it is those types of thoughts that proving your fixation on your generation.

Music, along with art, science, education, fashion, and technology evolves as our society do. It goes with the flow of mankind. Music is a forever changing force conveying our moods and emotions. But, its evolution has consumed us to the point of not being able to see it. It is a well-known fact each generation changes the music. But the changes are coming faster and faster.

When you have time, look up How Music Has Evolved in the past 70 Years. It is an article on Gizmodo.com, written by The Echo Nest and posted December of 2013. This is a small article, but it clearly shows music's evolution in regard to its' energy (higher), volume (louder), speed (faster), "bounciness" and "acoustic sound" (less and less). This article shows how music is directly related to the evolution of our society.

I try to keep my mind open to music. I take the time to actually listen to today's music. There should be some understanding between the generations. We should know why the youth today saying that artists like Lil Wayne, Justin Bieber, Drake, Kanye West, Justin Timberlake, Gucci Mane, Psy, Wale, Miley Cirus, Wiz Khalifa, Jay-Z and Beyonce are some of the greatest artist of all times. Some of you will read this book and won't even know who some of these people are. But, a young person, someone who did not seem to like rap music, told me that Lil Wayne would go into the music hall of fame. I looked at him as if they had lost all of their logical thinking.

But, after some soul-searching, I figured it out. They ARE some of the greatest performers of all times (according to this generation). The same thing went on in my generation among my peers. My generation felt performers like Dr. Dre (who really is not a doctor), Eazy-E, N Sync, Queen Latifa, Boy George, Ice Cube, Cindy Lauper, Devo and Eric B & Rakim, etc., were some of the greatest artist of all times (I still do). My mother and her peers was giving my generation the same look I gave the young man telling me about Lil Wayne. Check this out!! That child was giving me the same look I gave my mother. It was one of definite and assured confidence in what he was saying.

So what do we do?

Try to remember what the music did for you. We need to realize that each generation has a language. They have their own way of understanding that language. This is the language they use in their music. This generation, like all others before it has their own way of expressing themselves through art and music. Your generation was given the same privilege so we are not ones to judge the music. There is only one question to ask yourself. Am I open-minded enough to allow the next generation to enjoy their music without my opinion?

Chapter 10

THE NEWS

Maybe we should, as a society, try to focus on the positive aspects of news as opposed to the negative. Then the media will change their race for negative news to a race to see who is doing good things in the world.

In the past, it was the most reliable source of information you could possibly get. But, is the news reporting on the world or is the world imitating the news? How is something determined to be newsworthy? Is it viewer ratings, sponsors, how many hits on YouTube, likes on Facebook, or followers on Twitter and Instagram. Is this what the world has come to?

With the exception of spiritual leaders, reporters of the news are supposed to be some the greatest keepers of mankind. It is their job to inform us of what is happening in the world. The news has the power to make great changes within today's society with what they consider newsworthy. Over time what has become exciting news is always on the negative side? What is always at the top of the news? Murder, rape, war, violence, corruption, scandal, political grandstanding, and dishonest business tactics. Why do this stuff dominate the television? What happened to all the positive things in the world? Is it for the ratings?

Is what they are showing all we want to see?

There is a powerful Psychology Today article online called [5]Why We Love Bad News by Ray Williams. In it, he asks, "Is the media negative?" He concurs, "Media studies show that the bad news far outweighs good news by as much as seventeen negative news reports for every good one." My dear reader, this was reported in 2010. Do you think it has gotten better or worse?

This has become a vicious cycle. We've all heard the

expression that life imitates art, or is it the other way around. Today, who is telling the truth? That question was asked because of the competitive nature of what is considered the news. Especially with Twitter and Facebook being the forerunners of how we receive the news. Is television news competing with digital news? And, since we are more eager (according to studies) to take interest in negative news, does it become a question of who has the worst story? The Pew Research Center for the People & the Press is a great website to visit. Go to their site and view the research. It will give you some idea of our reaction to the news and vise versa.

So what do we do about it? Turn off the news? We know that's not possible.

Maybe we should, as a society, try to focus on the positive aspects of news as opposed to the negative. Then the media will change their competition for negative news into a race to see who is doing the most positive things in the world. We are the ones who have to change the trend. Let us make positivity more newsworthy. It is difficult, but possible. Turn away from negative news. Stop letting bad news plague our psyche, work, relationships, children, family, neighborhoods, cities, etc....

This chapter is a prime example of the chain of reactions that has been mentioned throughout this book. Check it out:

Bad News + Negative Emotions = Bad Mood
Bad Mood + Negative Interaction = Bad Relationship
Bad Relationships + Negative Intentions = Bad News

This is what we consider newsworthy...our bad moods and relationships. Ask Yourself: Would I prefer more positive information within the media or are you happy with negativity all around you?

We wake up and get ready for our day. The first thing we do is turn on the television or radio for the news. We go to our computers or phones to see what is happening on Twitter, Facebook and Instagram. Subliminally, we are mentally plagued with the murder, violence, war, and the degradation of just about anyone. Oh, sure...there is a sprinkle here and there about someone helping or saving someone. There may be a story about a new community center opening. But, on a daily basis, there are hundreds if not thousands of people doing some great things in obscure, unknown and greatly populated places.

Scenario: For the past two weeks you have been hearing all over the television and radio that the gangs of Chicago has been having a violent war. Innocent people (especially children) and police are getting killed at an alarming rate. Every day there has been a report within your neighborhood and eight people was killed the night before. And, although you personally have not heard the gunshots, you know it's true because you saw the news trucks. Today, however, there is something different. You look out the window feeling something is happening in your neighborhood. What do you see...hard-core gang members. About a hundred of them. They are picking up the trash and cleaning up the streets. They have paint, brushes garbage cans, bags, brooms and shovels. It is early in the morning, about 7:30 am. You are looking out your window at the very same gang members the news reports on every day. With sagging pants and white T-shirts, they were beautifying the neighborhood. You immediately run to the phone and call the media. You tweet and take pictures for Facebook. Then you wait. What happens... absolutely nothing? You soon find out it is only big news to you and maybe the other people that live in your community. You do not see any news trucks, although you called, and you get a few likes on Facebook. You begin to feel as if it was a dream and you were the only one to witness such a powerful and positive thing. After some time and no responses, what you witnessed falls to the back of your mind and you feel as if you now hold a precious secret. You ask yourself why the news people didn't show up? Why was I the only one excited about this?

When turn on the news, do we look for the feel-good stories to put a smile on our face, like the true account in the scenario? How many of us is quick to report the positive information when we encounter it?

With the reality and talk shows bombarding the television, the only reliable source of worldly information is the News. It is the conduit for the information we all (regardless of nationality) rely upon to keep us knowledgeable of the current events. If that conduit (source) only spews out negativity, then it is what flows into the world. If we focus on the positive and make that the main source of information we seek, then the current flow will change.

Chapter 11

THE LAW

This chapter is not to bash officers or to criticize the law or those who practice law. Hopefully, those individuals mentioned will understand that the few make you all look bad.

I know you will consider me quite bold with the inclusion of this chapter. But again, the words said within this chapter are of my own opinion. There is no need for you, to become upset, especially if the content does not pertain to you.

I was driving down the street one day…I decided to put this chapter in based on what I saw. I saw a police officer stop at a red light and go through as if it had changed to green. Now an officer would say that he/she had an emergency or a call. To me, it is a legitimate reason why the police officer decided to go through the red light. I have a question for every police officer. Why didn't the officer turn on the siren? This is something I see officers of the law do all the time. It is one of the many things this author has personally witnessed. Many of you have seen officers of the law displaying actions that would be considered illegal if you did the same thing.

This chapter is not to bash officers or to criticize the law or those who practice law. Hopefully, those individuals I just mentioned will understand that the few make you all look bad. The average citizen looks to law keepers and makers for our safety and protection. A salutation goes to each and every one of you, but I have a question.

What is with the "do as I say and not as I do" attitude so many of you have? This does not pertain to all of you of course, but you should ask yourself if the people you are sworn to serve and protect respect and trust you.

Scenario: A man pulls into his driveway. The automatic door opener to the garage is broken. He has to physically open the garage door from inside the house. He decides that, because it is cold outside, he will leave his teenage son (with special needs and wearing a school uniform) and his dog in the nice warm vehicle. He walks through his living room, past the kitchen, down the stairs and heads straight for the garage door. By the time he gets there, he hears loud voices. Fear strikes him as he remembers his son and dog are outside. As he lifts up the garage door, he quickly notices two police officers with guns drawn on his son. He comes out and says, "what is going on?" The officer, not yet realizing the situation quickly, asks him if this was his house. The man says yes....

At this point lawmakers, what should the officers do? They have clearly made a mistake. Should the officers give the man a sincere apology and tell him there was a suspicious character in the area. That they were just investigating and assure the man of his safety?

Well, here is what happened (and yes, like the rest of the scenarios, this one is true). The officer chose not to answer any of the man's questions. He only wanted to know why the officers approached his vehicle with their guns drawn. What did they see to make them suspicious?

Instead of being a true officer of the law and comforting the man by letting him know that it was an honest mistake, he decided to coldly wave the man off. He yelled at him to go inside his house with no explanation whatsoever. Instead of taking his family inside the house, he decided to take his son to his grandmother's house and go to the police station to file a report. The officers scared his son to tears.

Well, lawmakers...upholders and protectors of society.

Is that man (and his sons') faith in the law strengthened, or weakened? Should you, as people within the business of law enforcement, care about what those officers did? What were the consequences of their actions?

A personal letter to the police from a private source:

Dear Mr. Policeman

You said that you are here to protect and serve. I do not feel very safe. Please do not be mad at me Mr. Policeman, but at this point you scare me more than the criminals. At least with the criminals there are ways that I can defend myself. I cannot say that I can do the same with you. I would have never thought that I would have to. When you stop me, I am not confident that you will be fair, unbiased and follow all of the rules... Maybe...if I am a certain color or gender.

As you approach me Mr. Policeman I cannot help but wonder about what type of mood is you in. Are you one that does not like women? Are you one that does not like men? Are you racist? Are you mean? Are you drunk or high? Did you have a bad day, and now you are about to take it out on me? Are you trying to reach your quota? Are you a criminal yourself? Did you forget your oath, or better yet do you believe in your oath?

I am sorry Mr. Policeman, but this is what comes across my mind as you approach me. Not the situation that has caused you to be in my presence.

Now I fully understand that your job is among the toughest in the world, but if I am not mistaken, you knew that when you took the position. I depend on you to protect me from those of the world that is meant to destroy. I will admit Mr. Policeman I am not perfect. If I commit a crime, then by all means punish me accordingly. But please let the punishment fit the crime and I believe it is supposed to be a learning experience. I thought that with all of your training and equipment you knew exactly what to do in any situation. I was taught in school that you are fearless, understanding and true... a great protector from evil... superhero like. If that is not true, then I apologize for the mistaken identity. From what I see on the news, and from what I have experienced, I'm afraid of you. Is that right? When did you become so deadly? Who do I trust? Do I take the law into my own hands and protect myself? You tell me Mr. Policeman.

Sincerely
Afraid for my Life

Chapter 12

ROAD RAGE

Road rage has been a part of my life. I was a "road rager", always running late for an appointment or work... or to put it plainly, in a rush!

Have you ever wondered where it comes from?

The term road rage was not even heard of until the late 80's when there was an unusual amount of freeway shootings in Los Angeles, California.

What exactly is road rage?

Wikipedia states that: Road rage is aggressive or angry behavior by a driver of an automobile or another road vehicle. Such behavior might include rude gestures, verbal insults, deliberately driving in an unsafe or threatening manner, or making threats. Road rage can lead to altercations, assaults, and collisions that result in injuries and even deaths. It can be thought of as an extreme case of aggressive driving.

Since road rage start at the beginning of time, I wanted to find out more. I found a government website. It was the [6]National Center for Biotechnology. Now I will not go on about the article, that is why I provided the website. But, if I read it correctly it said, "up to one-third of community participants report being perpetrators of road rage".

Now I can very well admit. Road rage has been a part of my life. I was a "road rager", always running late for an appointment or work... or to put it plainly, in a rush!

Of course, there are plenty of medical studies and signs talking about road rage, but, how much stress do it actually cause? You are blaring your horn, yelling at traffic, jumping from lane to lane and worst of all tailgating. You know, when a car gets extremely close to the back of another vehicle.

What about a traffic jam? No one is thinking of how we can get traffic moving. Instead, you are thinking about you. And how you are not moving fast enough. But, how many times do you allow proper merging of vehicles? Are you obeying the rules of the road? Are you allowing enough space between you and the vehicle in front of you?

Rush... rush... rush... rush. One huge problem we have. Road rage is a prime example of how little we care for each other.

It could be said that we have all asked ourselves, "where does the time go?" Grant it, time is precious and goes by quickly. If we do not watch out, it will get away from us. But, is your time worth another person's life?

You are handling a weapon. A vehicle can be destructive and murderous if not handled properly.

Now for the sake of this chapter, think about it. How many accidents would be avoided, if every time you got behind the wheel of a car, bus, truck, plane, etc., you treated it as if you were carrying a dangerous loaded gun. Would you drive it recklessly?

The driving force behind road rage from personal observation is stress. I mentioned previously how we are always in a rush about something. It can be as simple as going to the store before it closes. We have all seen car fly past you almost causing an accident. You see them turn into the parking lot of the store or restaurant a block ahead. If you are the one who almost got hit, how did that make you feel? Or, have you ever rushed to the store? What if you were in a bad mood?

Rushing + Bad Mood = Road Rage

The rushing is a simple matter of bad planning. We know this...I certainly do, I will admit.

> On a side note: Why we don't have mandatory planning and scheduling classes. Can it be taught in the elementary educational systems? Just asking. If there is a school out there that has this, please make yourselves known and share your plan.

Anyway, it's the bad mood part that fuels the road rage.

We know it exists in all of us. In chapter 2, I stated, "when we wake in a bad mood, we can carry it throughout the day". This includes carrying it while driving. But you know that.

One-day, while in the middle of a road rage situation, it came to me that road rage has become some sort of filtration system for my own frustrations.

Just scream, cry, or yell it out!

Did you know it was good to occasionally scream? It is true. Look it up. Try the [7]Huffington Post. There is a good article about stress relieving techniques.

There are million of ways to reduce stress. But I want to talk about screaming only. Some days you feel like an unhappy two-year-old. Many of us do not know how to calm our emotions down. Some say breathe slowly, but sometimes it does not quiet the voices in your mind. Try this (only if you are physically able). Go somewhere very private. Away from family, friends, co-workers...people period. Once you are by yourself, have a fit. If you can, kick, scream, cry, or yell out all that is wrong with yourself and any thing else. Act like a spoiled toddler (please do not hurt yourself). Get it off your chest, that's how you are feeling anyway. It is far better doing it that way, than behind a vehicle. What do you think?

Just ask yourself this...If I am being my brother's keeper, how can I put so many lives at risk because I am either running late, mad or even worse...both?

The Reflection Page

Here is where you check your personal mirror and write down what you see about yourself.

Subject: Controlling My Anger Around Others.

In my mirror, I see:

Chapter 13

LAZINESS

Investing in your emotions is one of the greatest gifts you can give to your fellow man. It involves actual genuine caring for your family, co-workers, friends, associates and even enemies.

It can come in many forms, not just physical. Laziness is not a person just lying in bed or on the couch all day watching television. It is not your co-worker making the least amount of effort at work. Nor is it a matter of someone not picking up behind himself or herself. Did you know that laziness can manifest itself within an emotional or even mental state?

Physical vs. Emotional vs. Mental

What is your opinion? Do you think mental laziness cause physical and/or emotional laziness? Or, is it the other way around? Do the three play a role with each other? Or, are they three different formulations of laziness and should be worked on individually?

Hopefully, most of us know that before we are physically or emotionally lazy, mental laziness is already well set in place. Before any physical activity can manifest, or any emotional strength is to be acquired, there has to be some mental preparation. That is when you talk to yourself about your own limitations. You say from within if, "you can", or "you can't". The same is said for emotional laziness. It starts with the mind. Again...it is what you tell yourself.

The scary thing about mental strength being the first stop towards growth is that many of us do not follow (or listen to) our "first mind". Initially we hear a voice within telling us if something is right or wrong, good or bad. We will trust everything except our "first mind". But, when we don't follow it, the door to doubt and fear is quickly opened.

It can be safely said that the stronger you are mentally, the stronger you become physically and emotionally.

In been true to yourself, have you ever asked how your own personal laziness affect the people in your life? Or, are you emotionally lazy in your relationships? Have you checked how much mental effort you put in a learning situation? Well, I am so pleased to say, the human body is amazing. We have the uncanny ability to physically, emotionally, and mentally turn things around (heal ourselves), when things get "out of whack". But, it takes a huge amount of power from inside.

> Lazy: Unwilling to work or use energy. Characterized by lack of effort or activity. Showing a lack of effort or care.
> American Standard Dictionary

We all know about physical laziness and the damage it causes, but emotional and mental laziness are the worst types. I will explain why. The most hurtful when dealing with an emotional/mentally lazy person is, the uncaring disposition. You realize your needs are not a priority no matter how much they say they love or believe in you.

Emotions drive a person to move forward. It is usually second within the hierarchy of making decisions (depending on the person). Typically we start with logic and reason. That is the mental preparation part mentioned earlier. After something becomes logical, our emotions soon kick in and push us toward our final decision. Only to be stopped by your physical limitations. When laziness is in the picture however, that emotional push does not exist. Once the lack of care is in the picture, don't expect the consequences to be considered.

Investing in your emotions is one of the greatest gifts

you can give to your fellow man. It involves actual genuine caring for your family, co-workers, friends, associates and even enemies...yes, I said enemies.

If you notice I put the act of genuine caring in bold. Why did I do that? Well, what is the act of genuine caring?

It is truly paying attention to your mate, family member, good friend or associate when they have a bad attitude. With great care, you set out on the journey of finding out the problem. When you are not being your brother's keeper, your ego takes over. It automatically will tell you that the problem has nothing to do with you. Many of us take the "they always have an attitude" route. But, few of us find out why. Having that type of mentality is the slothful way of handling someone's bad disposition? It's an easy road to not dealing with the problem at hand.

In general, people sometimes forget that, we take our problems out on the person that is closest to us. Knowing this small bit of information, do you make a concerned effort to ask what the problem is?

Have you ever said, "what did I do now?" or "you always have an attitude when I see you". Well, a statement like that does nothing but ensue an argument or make the attitude worse. To them, you are assuming they will get over it regardless to how bad their problem is. It is the emotionally/ mentally lazy person that has these thought processes. It would be better to be truthful and simply say you do not want to deal with it. So O.K....

Let us say that, a person you love grievance has something to do with you. Ask yourself, how do I handle this? Can I maintain a civilized (yes I said civilized, because your feelings are hurt) conversation with this person to find out what the problem is? Is what they have to say important enough for me to actually listen? Once I find out the problem, can I drop my ego enough to make a heartfelt effort to change?

What if their discontent has nothing to do with you? If

you say that you truly care for the well being of this person, what type of emotional and/or mental energy have you placed into helping? Am I being a true, positive, and vital component within solving the issue at hand?

Now, instead of asking some hard questions about "self", you always have the alternatives. You can take the emotionally lazy path. When problems arise, you can instantly pull the uncaring you out and say that there is nothing wrong with you. According to this version of you, they're the ones with the problem and they need to drop it. You can also take the mentally lazy route, in which any consideration for anything is too much of a hassle and you tune out. The choice is yours.

Staying away from laziness (emotional or otherwise) falls directly in line with being your brother's keeper. It is putting your best foot forward, taking the high road and thinking about the consequences of our actions. Are those some of the acts you practice for those you genuinely care for? If the answer is no, then maybe (and this is between you and you), that act of laziness is something you should be working on. This is something that should be done, not only for you, but also for the happiness and well being of everyone involved with you.

Chapter 14

LYING AND CHEATING

Today, social media has made it is very easy for us to wallow in a state of low self-esteem.

Why do we lie and cheat? I mean, think about it. We're unfaithful to our spouses, tell lies to our loved ones, cheat on our taxes, funds, and bills. We're often untruthful to our bosses, and so-called friends. We can be deceptive with our diets, while playing games, and doing our work. We (meaning society) often look for a shortcut, which in a sense cheats everyone involved.

This chapter is not to chastise the reader, nor is it designed to appear hypocritical because I'm speaking to myself as well. BUT, it is designed to get you to think. I mean really think, about the consequences of your actions. There is a heavy chain reaction that goes along with both lying and cheating. The chain usually ends with someone getting hurt, mentally, physically and/or emotionally. The very first thing you should ask yourself is this. How honest am I with myself?

Using this very important question is the starting point of an extremely difficult, but highly rewarding, road to true honesty. Unless you are a vindictive, malicious and soulless individual, most of us lie or cheat out of fear. This could be a fear of hurting someone's feelings, failing, losing, or fear of the consequences to the plain ol' truth.

> Fear: An unpleasant emotion caused by the belief that someone or something is dangerous, likely to cause pain, or a threat; A mixed feeling of dread and reverence; A feeling of anxiety concerning the outcome of something or the

safety and well being of someone; The likelihood
of something unwelcome happening.

Fear can be a killer. It causes stress. Fear is the foundation
for a fragile house of lies when you build upon it. It is also the
one thing that most of us cannot control. We can, however,
manage our fear by initially recognizing it. Most of the
things we cheat for or lie about "save face". Meaning, we
don't want to look bad or face our mistake.

First, there has to be an understanding that lying and
cheating is a direct reaction to an action. Start asking yourself
if the actual act of lying, or the circumstance in which
you cheat, is worth the consequences of the reaction. The
consequences show its ugly head when the truth reveals itself.
When we lie or cheat, it is a conscious decision, no matter
how much we try to work our way around that fact. They
are also learned skills in which, the more you do it, the better
you are at it. With these skills however, you must know that
the better you are at it, the greater the negative repercussion.

Now, what about people that lie uncontrollably or for
no other reason than to lie? Or, those that cheat even when
they are winning? I am no physician by any means but, from
my close experience with compulsive liars and cheaters (and
it has been quite a few), I realize that they suffer from some
form of low (very low) self-esteem. Their soul survival is
based on lies and if the world found out the truth about who
they really are, then their life would diminish.

Today, social media has made it is very easy for us to
wallow in a state of low self-esteem.

Let's us take a peek at Facebook. Now it can be a great
source of inspiration and information. Businesses can expand
with advertising and long lost friends/family can reconnect
at any given time with their phones and/or computers. But
how many of us, in all honesty, is 100% truthful of what
is said on Facebook? Along with all of the positive aspects

of social media, there is the same, if not greater amount, of negativity. And this is excluding the thieves, predators and pedophiles. We're just talking about the liars...those speaking of their "dream life". We all know them or heard about them.

How many of us have 50 or more friends on the computer, but two or three that we see face to face. Or, 300 people that like your post, but, only one person allowed to know the real you. Ups and downs included. Do we know people who speak of great things, formidable accomplishments, etc., but, truly sit at home on the couch all day? What would come of that person if there were no such thing as Facebook? Do you think that they would be forced to get their life together? I can go on forever about how social media makes it easy for us to revel in low self-esteem, but you get the picture.

How to tell when someone is personally lying to you.

- Demeanor or voice radically changes.
- Avoids saying "I".
- Grooming gestures.
- Has an answer for everything.
- Fidgets and fusses for no reason.
- Proclaims honesty repeatedly.
- Throat-clearing or swallowing.
- Face touching: your face itch when we lie
- Pursed lips: your mouth gets dry. Pursing the lips adds moisture.
- Excessive sweating: nervous about the lie.
- Blushing: mainly women
- Head shaking: denying their own statement

Did you know that you can easily detect if someone is lying to you simply by paying attention to their eyes? The eyes are the true windows to the soul. This chart will show you how. Below are the natural eye movements for a right-handed person (just flip for a left-handed person).

Looks to Their Right
(your left)

Looks to Their Left
(your right)

Lying	**Truthful**

Looking up and to the right: lying about what they saw.

Looking up and to the left: remembering what they saw.

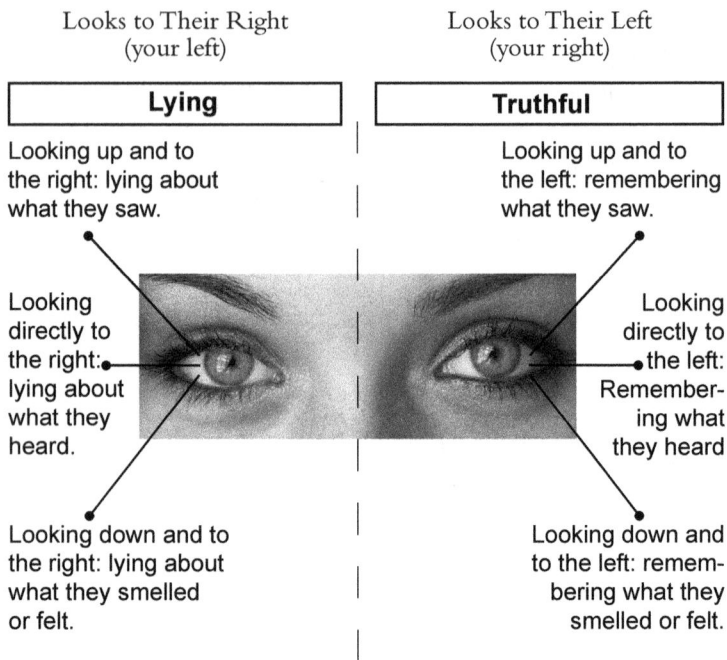

Looking directly to the right: lying about what they heard.

Looking directly to the left: Remembering what they heard

Looking down and to the right: lying about what they smelled or felt.

Looking down and to the left: remembering what they smelled or felt.

- Eyes darting back and forth: They feel uncomfortable about the lie.

- Rapid blinking: Stressed about lying.

- Closing eyes for more than one second at a time: contemplating the lie.

Chapter 15

SEX: IS IT LOVE OR LUST?

Knowing sex is an act, a skill, a learned tool to be used as needed, will help us to determine if we are experiencing love or lust.

We place entirely too much emphasis on sex. Just about everything has some type of sexual reference involved with it. Unknowingly, the way we dress, talk, walk, act and build relations with one another has some form of sexuality added.

Sometimes I do not understand how WE have allowed it to become such a force within OUR lives. People actually lie, cheat, steal and kill for sex as if it is a rare and unusual thing. It has toppled dynasties and caused wars! It is told to us in our youth that it is a precious, emotional and beautiful moment in our lives shared with another. We have to understand something: During the expression of pure love between two people, the precious part is the emotions experienced, not the physical act of sex.

We as a society act as if it is something brand new...fresh off the market. A man will look at an attractive woman walk pass him and act as if it is something that he has never seen before. That is until the next attractive woman walks pass... and the next... and then the next. A woman will see a handsome, muscular man and act as if he is a fine piece of rare art. She will take his image, carry it within her brain and use it for every occasion when needed (hint, hint, ... strippers).

Here's an equation for you the reader. Answer it and see what you come up with. The answer may surprise you.

Your Life − Sex =???

What would happen if we took the sexual notion out of our daily lives and based our decisions on such things like merit, qualifications, personality and actual facts?

The following is what I call, food for thought. They are everyday situations that would go very different if sex was taken out the equation.

That first Date: If the possibility of a sexual encounter was not the goal, then we would actually have to focus on a person's personality, likes and dislikes, wants and needs. These would be the determining factors while deciding if this is the person for you. The object of their physical features would not be an issue. Your attraction to them would be based on what he/she has on the inside. On the flip side, what do you think the results of the first date would be, if you showed the real you (not the representative self), without any type of sexual reference or provocative actions?

That interview for the perfect job: Did you ever notice that, getting ready for a job interview is like getting ready for a date? The type of clothing may be different, but, compare how much time you spend on what to wear as opposed to how qualified you are. Do you pick out a decent outfit (you know neat, clean and appropriate), and then spend the rest of the time researching the company you are interviewing for? Or, do you spend most of your time picking out the outfit you look best in? Why spend so much time on what you look like?

Boy-Girl Friendships: Why is it so hard to believe that males and females cannot be "best friends" (i.e. besties), without some sort of sexual actions being involved? The reason a woman and man become the best of friends is because they can receive all the benefits of a companion without the element of sex being an issue. It is a step above a friend with "benefits". It is a dis-heartening thought that our society fails to realize the appealing part of a male/female friendship. Sex is not involved. Somehow, there is a deep level of trust between them. It is based solely on each individual's natural characteristics. For some reason, they accept each other regardless of faults. This friendship can last forever with the exception of outside intruders constantly accusing them of being intimate. Ironically, sex actually tears the relationship apart and the friendship ends.

Scenario: You and your male/female friend have known each other since (in your mind) the beginning of time. You and he/she went to school together. Every since the first day you guys spoke on the playground there was a connection. Throughout the years you two seem to fall out of touch, only to find each other again. It has been about 10 years since you have seen or spoke to your friend. During that time, you've gotten married and had children. You mentioned him/her to your spouse, but they've never met. One day you and your friend see each other. Things pick up between the both of you as if you were still on the playground. He/she begins to come around a lot to hang out with you. Although the friendship is completely innocent (no form of intimacy involved), your spouse begins to show signs of jealousy and mistrust. Your spouse cannot believe that you and he/she can be strictly friends for such a long time. According to your spouse, it is possible to be best friends with same sex, but never the opposite sex. There has to be some form of sexual tension between the two of you. So, as a result, your spouse asks (maybe even demands) that you not spend so much time with your friend. You notice that it is causing a riff within your marriage. Your spouse is not willing to get to know your friend and now you are placed in the middle. You are forced to make a decision.

What would you do if you were in this situation?

Why is the spouse jealous?

Is this a trust issue?

Do you forsake your spouse?

Do you let go of your friend?

There are a million questions that can be asked about this scenario. But, in a perfect world, the friend and spouse would also become friends. Jealousy and mistrust would not manifest its ugly head. What if the thought of a sexual encounter between the friends never existed? Do you think the spouse would be jealous? Or, what if you are the spouse… would you be jealous and mistrusting?

The Intimate Relationship: How many of us been in a relationship we intend to be purely sexual? Have you ever wondered how it gets out of control? Why did someone get hurt? Why did feelings develop from the other person and not you? Or visa versa, why did you develop feelings when you knew it was only about sex? Why did it go on for so long?

We fail to realize that, you are getting to know the person as we spend those intimate moments together. Unless you get together with someone and have sex without words or spending actual time, then maybe you can get away with it. We often confuse good sex as a characteristic trait. Sex is not a sign of good character. Just because a person is good in bed, does not mean they are a person of good conscience or has a kind heart. Sex is a skill. It is something that can be learned and mastered. It can be used as a form of true expression or a tool of manipulation.

Recognizing what sex actually is, will probably remove a great deal of confusion within our lives. Knowing sex is an act, a skill, a learned tool to be used as needed, will help us to determine if what we are experiencing in an intimate relationship is love or lust. With this realization, we can eliminate notions of sexuality, sexual connotations, sexual agendas, sexual motivations and/or sexual manipulations from our daily lives.

Maybe we can get down to the actual business of getting to really know one another. We can become friends and better mates, partners, or all-around better judges of character if sex wasn't in the picture.

~~~~~~~~

IS IT LUST?

You or the person you are involved with is totally focused on the body...Or looks. The goal is sex not conversation. Therefore, finding out the person's favorite color or food is nowhere on the priority list unless you are frigid enough to use that ammunition to get the sex. Then the relationship becomes a fantasy and real feelings are never discussed. If they are not lying to you...you are lying to them. You are lovers in the physical sense, but not actual friends. You leave after sex. There is no cuddling or breakfast the next day.

IS IT LOVE?

You are not focused on sex and want to actually spend time together. Sex is a bonus. You get lost in conversations and you honestly listen to each other's feelings. Because you want to know everything there is to know about that person, questions constantly plague your mind. Time is forgotten or secretly unwarranted because you make each other very happy and peaceful. He or she begins to motivate you to become a better person and you soon get to know the family and friends. You feel secure about sacrifices because he or she is worth it to you.

Chapter 16

ARROGANCE VS. CONFIDENCE

If you are confident, then you have no problem asking yourself questions about anything. You can check your ego enough to make sure you are not crossing over into arrogance.

Are you arrogant? Or confident?

M any people often ask what is the difference. Even though they have similar characteristics, they are definitely not the same. Both contain self-assurance. A sense of your own self-importance or value of your abilities. That is where the similarities end.

Are people comfortable around you?

When you are arrogant your sense of self-importance is greatly over exaggerated. The impression of you being better than everyone else is not based on actual success. An arrogant person gloats. They let all those around know of their successes whether they are real or not. They constantly tell everyone about their abilities regardless if they actually have them or not. They take delight in the misfortunes of others and in fact, use those misfortunes as their own personal stepladders.

This is how an arrogant person gets ahead in life. They try to convince people that they are the S**T in any given situation and always make their presence known. The most important characteristic of an arrogant person is that they lack the ability to be empathetic.

Empathy: The ability to understand and share the feelings of another.

A person who is confident has the same sense of self-importance as someone who is arrogant. The difference here is, a person who is confident gains it based on their accomplishments. Usually, someone who is confident does not believe they are better than others. They know they are great at what they do, but there is no need to publicize it. A confident person has the attitude that you are the best you, and they are the best them. In fact, they will encourage others to be equally successful. They know their limitations and do not try to exceed their abilities in order to look better than they really are. Confidence goes hand in hand with empathy. With empathy, comes teamwork. Teamwork is leads to success for everyone involved.

After this explanation about the difference from my own understanding (and hopefully yours, so we can be on the same page), at the beginning of this chapter I asked a question: Are you confident, or arrogant? Remember, you and you alone is reading this book, and the question only has to be answered within yourself. If you are arrogant, then this chapter will offend you, because I asked you to question yourself. That is one of the traits of an arrogant person - the blatant disregard of others' opinions or questions. If you are confident, then you have no problem asking questions about anything. You check your ego enough to make sure you are not crossing over into arrogance.

Speaking of the ego, that is the basis of this chapter. Hopefully you will take notice and check the size of yours. Is it so big that, you cannot bring yourself to believe there are others out there with skills and opinions? Do you say to yourself on a constant basis, no one can tell me better than I already know? If so, then not only is this writer surprised that you are taking the time to read this chapter, but the book, period. That means that you are practicing the reverse action of going from arrogance to confidence, which is a part of being your brother's keeper.

Chapter 17

OUR BELIEFS

Are you really showing true concern for their soul or are you just mad because they don't believe as you do. If you are mad because their view is different, then you are just being arrogant.

This chapter is probably going to upset a lot of people. There is no need. I know this is a touchy subject. Originally it was not going to be in this book, but I decided to be brave. What can I say?

There are so many forms of beliefs, religious or otherwise, all over the world. I mean no disrespect to any of them, but there is a very serious question that needs to be asked.

Why do we become so furious with someone or a group of people having a different belief system than our own?

What we believe in is based on personal experiences, geographical region, nationality, influences, etc., throughout a person's life. Some of us believe the way we enter the world is the way we exit... alone. It is true we all have different ideologies about where we end up when we die. Ask yourself, if it is your right to become angry and judgmental because they do not share the same belief (or vise-versa)?

> Conversion: the fact of changing one's religion
> or beliefs or the action of persuading someone
> else to change theirs.

Some would say, "yes". Have you ever heard someone say, "I have the right to be angry because what I believe is the ultimate truth and all should believe as I do...."? Some feel they are to get the message out. But, when it turns violent, it becomes all about conversion. How many people you can get to believe as you do, by any means necessary.

When it comes to a person's belief, things can get really nasty. The anger can be as mild as an elderly woman in a Baptist church who scoffs and gossips about the direction the congregation is taking. To, all out, full scale, deadly and historically changing wars between countries, believing in the same creator but practice different forms of worship.

Because what you believe comes from within, someone else believing differently strikes a blow to the ego. Can it be because a different belief can only mean:

> You are wrong and has been misled.
> They are wrong and is trying to mislead you.

The anger comes from the not knowing. Our egos play a big role in what we choose to believe in and it does not do well with making mistakes. Our arrogance does not allow us to drop the ego and admit being wrong. The not knowing of your pending judgment (death) leads to a great fear that is brought out in the form of anger. This anger is then transferred quickly to the person or group of people challenging the validity of your belief.

I was told not to put this chapter in the book due to possible repercussions. It may provoke some to violence. But this book is designed for the reader to ask some hard-core questions. While doing research on religious violence, I came across the [8]Pew Research Center. This is a great website for valuable information. I would encourage you to visit the site. January of 2014, they reported that at least a third of the world is suffering from religious violence. Something needs to be done. The title of the story is [9]Religious Hostilities Reach Six-Year High. [10]Worldometers is also a great site to visit. This website has a population clock. In 2010, The Pew Forum conducted research, this chart (I created) is based on their statistics.

Pew Forum Research
World Population According to Religion

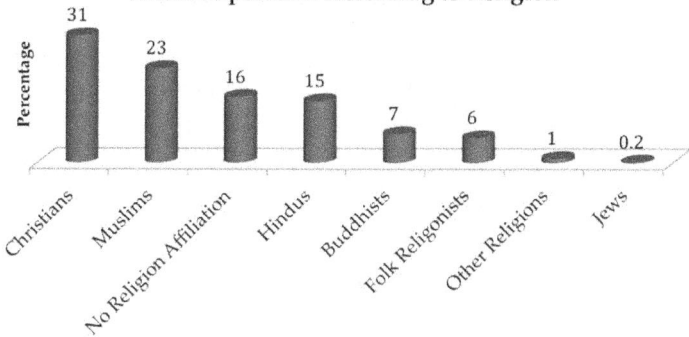

2010 world population of 6.9 billion

[11]*For more information.*

Because people was killing each other over their religious beliefs, congress passed the International Religious Freedom Act in 1998, "which affirms U.S. commitment to religious freedom, enshrined both in the United States Constitution and in numerous international human rights instruments, including the Universal Declaration of Human Rights (UDHR) and the International Convention on Civil and Political Rights (ICCPR). Official White House Response to Recognize [12]"SIKH" Genocide 30,000+ Killed in India During November 1984 - "Yes, It Is Genocide"

Getting angry and violent will not help you gain more followers. Anger only fuels insanity. If you are so secure and strong in what you believe in, then why do you get so irate. So much so, you come to the point of hurting someone? We all know we go to judgment alone. If you even believe there is a final judgment. So, why not leave another's belief between them and their maker. Are you really being your brother's keeper by showing true concern for their soul or are you just mad because they don't believe as you do. If you are mad because their view is different, then you are just being arrogant.

Now I know we have people in the world, who believe in stuff that transgress thru deceptive conversion and causes damage, (physical and mental) to other people. What is to be done about them? Technically, they have the right to practice what they believe in. But, in being the keepers of mankind (each other) we cannot allow the destruction of another human for any reason.

Chapter 18

PROCRASTINATION

The process of working on procrastination can be a trying experience. You go through some emotional truths about yourself. But once you are done, you will be proud of yourself.

I wrote this chapter for myself. With all the other chapters, I used other individuals and the pleasure of my experiences. This chapter is personal. It is my wish that, in helping myself with this chapter, I can share the wealth and help you.

Procrastination: To delay or postpone actions; put off doing something.

Have you ever wondered why people procrastinate? Or, do you even care? Have you ever ask yourself why you procrastinate. Even if you do not want to know the answer, ask anyway.

It took five years to write this book. For that, I apologize. I was not being my brother's keeper. I did not think about the consequences of my actions. I procrastinated. And, I will admit...this chapter was not put in until the very end. I was already finished with the book. After I was done, I wondered what took me so long. I did something I have been asking you to do throughout this entire book. I questioned myself with some hard-core questions. Was I just being lazy, or was it fear? Maybe I simply did not care enough.

The reason for my procrastination was this.

"I do not think I cared enough."

My procrastination came from fear. A fear that came from the need of acceptance by readers of this book. It caused me to be emotionally and physically lazy. Allowing my fear to supersede my obligation of being a brother's keeper to you.

When I first starting writing, I was saying, "I really hope I can help people with my little book". As I got further into writing, my ego set in. My mind and ego both began to tell me, "someday...people like Dr. Cornell West, Steve Harvey, and Oprah Winfrey will read my book and say that it helped so many people" Notice how my attitude and goals change once the ego came into play. After wasting time on dreaming about famous people, I started telling myself that I could not do it and that it will never happen. I was convinced. Doubt is another doorway to lazy town. Mental laziness set in and that led to physical and emotional laziness...hence the procrastination. To put it simple, I procrastinated because I was scared. I then realized it was my ego playing tricks on me. In the beginning, I did not care who read this book, as long as it helped someone. I lost sight of the initial goal. I soon checked my ego and went back to my first mind. I told myself that, "...its ok if Dr. West, Ms. Winfrey or Mr. Harvey don't read my book...as long as it's helpful in this crazy world".

Everyone that procrastinates has procrastinated or carries the seed of procrastination, from me to you, I say...STOP! It is ok. Take some time to form some bravery. Breathe slowly and think about your initial reasoning. Take some time and ask yourself,

Where did I go wrong?

When did I lose the drive?

Why am I so behind schedule?

Am I afraid of success?

Am I afraid of failure?

Do I have the energy to pick up from where I went wrong?

Do I have the energy to start over?

The only way you are going to fix the problem is to first find out where it comes from. And be honest with yourself. The process of working on procrastination can be a trying experience. You go through some emotional truths about yourself. But once you are done, you will be proud of yourself.

The Reflection Page

Subject: My Level of Procrastination

In my mirror, I see:

_____

_____

_____

_____

_____

_____

_____

_____

_____

_____

_____

_____

_____

_____

_____

_____

_____

_____

_____

_____

Chapter 19

THE BARREL OF CRABS SYNDROME

Crabs pull each other back into the barrel instead of using their claws to help each other...that way they all can get out... It becomes a malicious war complete with none of the crabs finishing the ultimate goal... getting out.

Think about a barrel of crabs caught fresh from the sea? As if they are aware of their fate, a crab will desperately attempt to escape from the barrel. This escape is to be achieved by any means necessary including the pulling down, climbing over and stepping on of the other crabs. It becomes a malicious war complete with none of the crabs finishing the ultimate goal...getting out the barrel. A crab will wait until another has almost escaped before yanking it back into the barrel, as if it is implying "you can't get out if I can't".

If you really pay attention to this act of nature (something that you can look up online), you may say something to yourself like, "why do they pull each other back into the barrel instead of using their claws to help each other...that way they all can get out". Now, if you decide to take the time and look up a barrel of crabs on the Internet I ask that you do something. Before you ask yourself that question, remove the barrel you see and imagine our world, then take the crabs out the picture and put in the human being then ask yourself the question.

Have you ever heard the term "having a crab mentality" or have someone said that about you? It is a term that is used to describe a kind of single-minded, selfish thinking person. Generally, it means that he or she (just like the crabs describe in the previous paragraph) is unwilling to allow someone to get out of a situation or to get ahead before they are able to. This stealth style mentality can strike at all levels of life, any place and at any time. Basically, being like a "barrel of crabs" or having the "crab mentality is a failure of collective thinking or a refusal to support certain investments, causes, ideas, etc., to the point of no one getting ahead. It is sad to say, but unknowingly the "crab mentality", which is the prominent way of thinking these days, has been particularly devastating to how we live among each other. This is just a though but, maybe…just maybe the world would be very different if the "barrel of crabs" syndrome never existed. Just think about the countless number of helpful organizations that did not get a chance to thrive and/or do not exist today due to the coworkers and partners tearing each other apart in order to get ahead. Do you have the mentality of a crab?

Many of us are not willing to admit that we do. It is ok because, as with most things that plague our lives fear is the basis for a "crab mentality" too. While trying to exist in today's world, there are so many things to be fearful about… our health, safety, family, etc. But, the "crab mentality" develops from the fear of not getting your due recognition. Who wants to put their hard earned money, or blood sweat and tears into something for the sake of seeing it grow? Maybe at some points in history we had that as a human race, but we are so afraid that the person that we help or support is going to leave us where we stand, that the sheer thought of helping that person, family member, organization, starting company, etc., quickly gets kicked out of your mind.

Just as quick as the thought of being left behind is formed within our mind, a judgment is made. Millions of reasons other than the truth form. We began to say to ourselves things like, "they are not prepared enough for me to help them", or "I can tell that they will not do as they say".

Chapter 20

THE BUTTERFLY EFFECT

Things may happen that are not in your control, but if your intent is not to cause harm, or if you are truly remorseful (deep from within) for your actions, then your karma can change.

To talk about the butterfly effect is to talk about karma. Some of us refuse to acknowledge the existence of karma, but that's not to say it doesn't exist. As I mentioned in the introduction, karma is simply a reaction to an action, which in turn causes a sort of a ripple type effect within the universe that somehow comes back to you... like a boomerang. Some scientists even affirm that karma exists.

Check out - www.apa.org/ monitor/2013/karma.aspx.

The word karma is Sanskrit, which means that it is an ancient word. Look up the history one day when you are bored. It is actually very interesting.

Now karma, no matter how much you try to deny it, is something that you cannot escape from. The ironic thing is that we do not have to be afraid of it because you have the power to control how it comes back to you.

Some of us deny karma because we do not understand it.

You can start with the fact that you are responsible for your actions. You are also responsible for the reactions to your actions and the consequences that are included. So, if you cause someone pain and start a negative cycle of events, then it is inevitable that it will come back to you. Remember, within the universe, we are our own individual worlds, and we all know that a world travels in a circle...which means it goes around and around. It may be unrecognizable, mainly due to the fact that it is in greater form.

Believing that karma does not exist can be causing damage to your own existence. Ask yourself, if karma does not exist then why are you faced with so many obstacles in your world. You may be saying to yourself that you have never caused anyone harm, but can you be certain of that fact?

Did you know that karma could spread in either a negative or positive fashion as well as physically, emotionally, mentally, and verbally? It travels in the form of what is called the butterfly effect. Just the thought of causing harm to someone else can release of bad karma. Now I don't know about you, but I kind of froze when I first discovered that little piece of information. I have never wanted to go so far as to kill someone, but I reflected on all the negative thoughts and bad intentions I had about others both large and small.

Part of the determination of your karma greatly depends on the intent. Things may happen that are not in your control, but if your intent is not to cause harm, or if you are truly remorseful (deep from within) for your actions, then your karma can change. That is why you can cause bad karma for yourself just from a thought that has bad intentions, so imagine if you acted upon those thoughts.

Chapter 21

PLAYING 20 QUESTIONS

I am just guessing, but these may be some of the questions traveling across your mind after reading this book. Have fun and play a game with yourself.

Did you ever play 20 Questions when you were a child? In case you have never heard of this past time activity, it is a classic game that has been played since the 19th century. One person thinks of an object and the others player have 20 chances to guess what it is. The rules for this version are a little different because you are playing it with yourself. Your personality is the object that you are trying to figure out. Get a pen and paper to write down your answers. Here are 20 questions for your conscience. You have only 1 chance to guess the answers (and be honest).

Ready Set Go!

1. Is there an area in my life where I feel out of control?_____

   _____

2. Am I a morning person or a night person?

   _____

3. Am I comfortable or uncomfortable in a disorderly environment?_____

   _____

4. Am I motivated or threatened by competition?_____

   _____

5. Do I find it easy to do things for other people rather than myself?_____

_____

6. Can I control my ego?_____

_____

7. Can I let go of control if it means the betterment of the situation?_____

_____

8. Do I work constantly?_____

_____

9. How do I truly feel about authority?_____

_____

10. Do I work well under pressure?_____

_____

11. What would my perfect day look like?____

_____

12. What steps do I have to take to get my perfect day?_____

_____

13. What's more, satisfying to me: saving time or saving money?_____

_____

14. Do I like to be in the spotlight or up front?_____

_____

15. Is my life "on hold" in any aspect?_____

_____

16. What energizes me? _____

_____

17. What takes my energy away?_____

_____

18. Do I get frustrated easily?_____

_____

19. Am I whole or is it something missing?___

_____

20. What accomplishment would make the biggest difference to my happiness?_____

_____

_____

_____

When you done answering these questions, go to www. truity.com. Go to the personality type page and write down the personality type you think you are based on your answers. Understand that this exercise is not a medical or self diagnosis of any kind. This is just a cool way to introduce yourself to your personality.

I have a_____personality.

ON A PERSONAL NOTE
Take some time to analyze your answers
write down your thoughts.

_____
_____
_____
_____
_____
_____
_____
_____
_____
_____
_____
_____
_____
_____
_____
_____
_____
_____
_____
_____
_____
_____
_____

Chapter 22

THE AFTERTHOUGHT

To be your brother's keeper is to work on being the best you so those outside of you do not have to suffer the consequences of your actions.

I got most of my information from personal experiences and real life. I also did some research to reassure my opinions, so I included websites and articles for you to search yourself. Everyone like reassurance and confidence in what you are reading. There are so many different books out there telling you that, everything will be ok if you take some time out for yourselves. And the age ole "you can do it". I cannot say those words because it is up to you. I can only try to help by sharing my knowledge and experiences with you. It is my way of trying to be my brother's keeper.

I've read self-help books. Some has helped me and some were not so beneficial. There was a misunderstanding of what the book is trying to tell me to do. I will always continue to seek self-improvement, but sometimes I get lost and forget. I will become utterly confused on my next steps.

I stop and breathe. Here is an exercise that I perform. Some may say that it can be a form of meditation. Maybe it can work for you.

Sometimes (not all the time), I wake earlier than normal to sit quietly and think. I do not think about what I have to do for the next hour, day or week, instead I imagine a big circular room that has file cabinets all around lining the walls. Each cabinet is labeled with factors of life. Work, home, health, love, family, friends, etc. Files and paperwork are all over the place. Then I imagine that I am sitting on the floor in the middle of the room organizing the paperwork. The pieces of papers, files and notes are the facts of my life and I am putting them where they should go.

That is it. Sometimes I do not know how long I sit...you may need to set an alarm. But most of the time this clearing of my mind helps me to stay focused.

During the writing of this book, individuals would ask me as I sent out samples, "What am I going to get out of it? What's the purpose of writing this?" If a conversation, discussion, debate, or if any person reading this book decides to take the time to think about the next man or anything of the sort has been sparked from the reading of any parts of this book, then the purpose is fulfilled. This book is designed so that any individual can begin the steps to gaining self-awareness...to get into the habit of asking themselves the hard questions...

And possibly coming up with some solutions...

Chapter 23

RACISM

No matter how much we try to deny, oppose, avoid, fight or ignore it. THE FACT IS.... WORKING TOGETHER has become detrimental to our survival.. It doesn't matter who you are.

So what can I say about racism that has not been said before. Nothing much. I wrote this chapter because of the moronic mentality of anyone that is racist these days. It is funny saying that in 2016, we still have a problem with any facet of any culture that walks upon this earth. Closely examine yourself in a mirror. Do you really want millions of you on earth? People that act like you. That has the same mentality and ideologies.

I is very sad and I pray for anyone who has not had the pleasure of getting to know another culture. Sometimes we choose not to learn about another culture because we get trapped in our own little box. Tasting another culture's food, familiarizing with their style of dress or understanding their thought processes when it comes to family and love, seems unfathomable. Somewhere along the lines of our growth, we are taught that what we do not understand has no validity.

Just like the crayons in a box, we are colorful. Remember when you were a child and you got the big box of crayons with all the colors? You were excited because you knew you were going to create a fantastic picture. One filled with life and vitality. Your choice of colors were unending.

Now, to give you a piece of history, when Crayola Crayons came out in 1903, there were eight colors. What if the company never developed another color? Lucky for us they chose to evolve because we would have some undeniably plain pictures using those same eight colors today 113 years later.

When you are choosing to engage in racism, you are saying that you only want one color...The color you are most comfortable with. Why on earth, would anyone want a plain life? Think of the people on earth like the Crayola Crayon box. We cannot take one crayon out the box and throw it away. Even the colors we believe to be ugly and out of place. Every color has its place and destruction of any of them would distort the actual picture of our growth.

With all the diseases, war, poverty, and destruction along with the problems we are facing with nature interchanging, decomposing, regrouping, and re-birthing, how do we even still have time to hate each other because of the color of our skin? Consider the "notion" that we are the most evolved of all other species. How do we allow something as simple as skin, interfere with our own evolution? We are the only ones with this problem. Start watching nature. Pay close attention to bears, birds, dogs, or any animal you choose and study its genealogy. Notice the different colors, breeds, and shades. Then, ask yourself if that species is hindering their growth because of physical differences? We don't get mad at birds and flowers for being so colorful. We marvel at them and say "Wow that is absolutely beautiful!" And yet we look at each other with such hatred and discuss. The Creator blessed us...The human species to be the most colorful of all but we inhibit our growth with something ridiculous like racism.

> Racism: prejudice, discrimination, or antagonism
> directed against someone of a different race based
> on the belief that one's own race is superior.

The way we treat each other sometimes makes me want to be an animal. We all come out of mother's womb without the choice of what we look like. Genetics tells us that. We know that there is no choice with the color of our skin, the slant of our eyes or how strait our hair is. We cannot control how full or thin our lips are. No matter how much we try with all the surgeries available to us. We are all designed with our own individuality. No two people are exactly alike unless you were born with an identical twin. And, since no two people are alike no two groups of cultures can be alike. It is against nature.

Above was the Webster definition of the word racism. Can you undeniably say to yourself that one culture of people is superior to the other? That is something none of us should even consider because, "A**holes come in all colors and everyone has one!" We can all get along and be proud of our heritage and culture. There is nothing wrong with that. However, to ensue hate, murder and utterly vile forms of behavior because you believe your culture is superior to any other culture shows great cowardliness. Some of us are willing to destroy this earth and everything in it for the sake of being right. We are the only species that was blessed with CHOICE. With this great blessing called CHOICE, we are actually opting to destroy each other because of imprudent things like the color of our skin, the nature of our hair, our culture, and what we believe in. Again, look at nature. The animals do not have the option of CHOICE and yet they do what they are supposed to do.

One of the silliest choices we as humans make is giving such eminent power to words and not actions. The "N" word is one word that baffles me. How can one word wreak so much havoc? I decided to look up the history of that word. YES! It actually has a history!

First thing I noticed while doing the research is the fact that the word did not have evil origins. Meaning, if you check the history of the word, you will find out that it was used to describe a color...

...Side note: Earlier I talked about Crayola Crayon and how they first came out with 8 colors in 1903. Well, it was in the 1400's when the Portuguese first encountered the people of West Africa so you can only imagine how many colors available to them.

The Portuguese stumbled upon the Bantu Tribe in Southern Africa while searching for routes to India. The Spanish word Negro is a derivative of the Latin word Niger which literally means black. The skin color of the people in the Bantu Tribe (especially at that time) was extremely dark. Almost to the shade of Black. So, that is how they were described. As Black...Or Negro.

The next thing I noticed was the interchangeable use of the word. Many different nationalities use different versions, spellings and meanings of the "N" word. It wasn't until humans of color started to get treated as animals that one version of the word stuck with the world. The negativity now attached to the word, originally being used to describe a color, was so devastating to us all that it has became taboo. So much so that in 2016 we simply say, the "N" word.

That word is just one of many stereotypical words used to describe a people. Most racial words used to describe the culture or physicalities of people has some type of history that started off positive but ended negative. It always boils down to our attachment to the word. We need to remember, if we decide to use racially motivated words, that it is the negative attachment to the word that you are using.

It is that negative mentality you are showing to other humans. Ironically, it is because of the stereotype. This is the vicious cycle we have fallen into. Ask Yourself: Have I fallen into the racial subjection of another culture?

You are angry about a culture of people and want them gone because of the stereotypes you hear. It is not actuality. It is what you hear.

So you use racially motivated, stereotypical words towards that culture. Which makes them angry and act out as you believe they would. When in actuality they are just angry at your misconception of them. Well, now you believe you have validation for your racial attitude when in actuality, you haven't completely looked at your part in the whole of it all. And the cycle continue going around and around.

Who wouldn't act out when they are being lied about constantly? Instead of allowing our ego to push our fears of the unknown into hatred, try having a five-minute conversation with someone of a different culture and you will find out that they have the same problems you do. Every culture has their share of murderers, rapist, thieves, and all around "bad" people. No culture can say that the entirety of their people is of one accord. So how can superiority of so-called "race" be an issue?

Superior: higher in rank, status, or quality; of high standard or quality; greater in size or power; above yielding to or being influenced by; having or showing an overly high opinion of oneself; supercilious.

Looking at that definition, ask yourself two questions. Which culture is truly superior to the other? And, is my culture of people truly superior to all other cultures? Remember, when you ask those two questions, think about my earlier phrase, "A**holes comes in all colors and everyone has one!"

Racism a product of the capitalism that grew from the use of slaves for the plantations of the New World. Today we use racism in order to create racial stereotypes on the basis of race, color, nationality, religion and other factors. It is 2015 and we are still judging people according to the color of their skin.

What are the symptoms of the "dis-ease" called Racism?

- Xenophobia: intense or irrational dislike or fear of people from other countries
- A need to socially, politically, and economically dominate other groups.
- A feeling that basic human rights for minority groups are "special rights."
- Historic patterns of prejudice, discrimination, colonialism, historic hostilities, and the slave trade.
- Ignorance of other cultures, religions, and values.
- Fear of sharing power with other groups of people.
- Isolationist and protectionist foreign policies.
- Laws and government policies aimed at preventing immigration of people of different cultures and religions.

Regardless of race, color, creed, age, sexual preference, financial status, choice of music, belief system (religious) or style of healthcare, we all have to live on this earth and breathe its air.

Chapter 24

THE LANGUAGE OF THE BODY

It is not always what you say, but how you say it. Body language is the key.

The face has a little more than 20 muscles. We use each and every one of them constantly, especially when we are in the process of expressing ourselves. Most of the time the reactions we receive as we are verbalizing something comes from the look on our face or better yet what our body's language is saying.

Why is it that two people can say the exact same statement to a group and receive completely different reactions? The answer is the body language shown as the statement was being said. One can say it with a smile and the other with a frown and the meaning of the statement can be taken into two totally different directions. Your facial expressions are the biggest part of your body's language.

Body language in my opinion is the loudest form of communication and yet it is the one greatly overlooked. Initially we pay attention to what is said by a person. The indifference or switch in our attitude comes when the body's language and what is being said does not match. Now, I will not go into the actualities of body language because, you reading this, are not ignorant. We all know when we are rolling our eyes, smacking our lips or huffing. What I will say however, is that or bodies gives the truest form of communication. Your body reveals the raw honesty of your feelings about any subject matter.

Earlier I mentioned that it was the most overlooked forms of communication. It just seems in my opinion, as if either, A.) We don't realize that we express ourselves with our bodies (predominately our face) or, B.) We believe that everyone we come in contact with is stupid and cannot recognize your true attitude about the subject at hand. Either way it is harmful (emotionally) to the person or people you are interacting with at that moment.

The question you have to ask yourself is...

Do I know my body language?

Most people will say "Yes!" This is a viable answer. Who knows you better than you right? I will be honest and say, "No. I am still learning." I thought I knew myself also, until I started to listen. It is much harder than we think to "know thy self." So many make it seem easy, but in truth it is NOT! It requires some things we choose not to do.

THAT IS RIGHT LADIES AND GENTLEMEN, you have to actually take a moment and listen to people when they say, "Your attitude is messed up." Or, "Hey! Why are you being so mean?" And the best one yet, "What's wrong?"

The common response instantly is one on the defensive. Why is that? Very few of us will actually acknowledge that what that person is saying may have some validity. In other words saying to yourself, "My attitude IS messed up."

Here is where the body language comes in. The person asking the questions of a concerning or curious nature is reading your body language. But, being the smart and self-aware person that you are instantly feels that person cannot know what they are talking about. Again, no one knows you better than you right?

Wrong.

When will it dawn on us that the person "analyzing" your body language is, "On the outside looking in." We are not robots and the person you are conversing with can tell when you actually have a conflict with the words that are coming out of your mouth. This is the great denial. We act as if the person cannot tell the difference when your shoulders slump or your voice raise or lowers in octaves.

How may arguments, disagreements, or fights have you witnessed because of miscommunication? Think about it. Many times the misunderstanding comes from how something was said and not what was actually said. You often hear the words, "I didn't mean to say it like that." Have you ever said those words? Have you ever wondered how you got involved in a particular argument? Did you ever think, it was how you said what you said? It may be the root of the argument. Oh! I forgot you have to drop your ego to do that. The other hard part when getting to know yourself.

That darn ego! You have to give someone the benefit of the doubt in saying that maybe they are right. No one wants to do that. But, that is what it takes in order to get to know yourself truly. This is why it is so hard. The ego will not let you stop and say, "I apologize. You are right. I'll do something about that."

Communication

The imparting or exchanging of information or news • A letter or message containing information or news • The successful conveying or sharing of ideas and feelings • Social contact • Means of connection between people or places, in particular • The means of sending or receiving information, such as telephone lines or computers: satellite communications • The means of traveling or of transporting goods, such as roads or railroads • The field of study concerned with the transmission of information by various means.

Majority of the subject matter of this book wraps itself

around communication. Our interactions with each other. We can fix the contempt and mistrust we have for each other. It starts with you. Can you do it? I think you can. Just work on you. That is what I am doing for you.

> "To be your brother's keeper is to work on being the best you so those outside of you do not have to suffer the consequences of your actions."

Peace

Reference

1. (http://psychcentral.com/blog/
    archives/2012/12/07/talking-to-yourself-a-
    sign-of-sanity/)

2. https://en.wikipedia.org/wiki/Intrapersonal_
    communication

3. www.livescience.com/14394-educational-
    achievement.html and read.

4. http://abcnews.go.com/2020/story?id=2463266

5. https://www.psychologytoday.com/blog/
    wired-success/201012/why-we-love-bad-news

6. www.ncbi.nlm.nih.gov/pmc/ articles/
    PMC2922361/

7. www.huffingtonpost.com/2013/04/09/
    stress-relief-tools-old-fashioned-
    remedies_n_3022241.html

8. www.pewresearch.org.

9. http://www.pewforum.org/2014/01/14/
    religious-hostilities-reach-six-year-high/.

10. www.worldometers.info

11. http://www.worldometers.info/ world-
    population/#religions.

12. https://petitions.whitehouse.gov/response/
    speaking-out-against-and-preventing-violence-
    based-religious-affiliation

www.ingramcontent.com/pod-product-compliance
Lightning Source LLC
Chambersburg PA
CBHW072011040426
42447CB00009B/1585